TURKISH

Phrase book

Bengisu Rona

School of Oriental and African Studies
University of London

Series Editor: Carol Stanley

D0317776

BBC Books

BBC Books publishes a range of products in the following languages:

ARABIC	GREEK	POLISH
CHINESE	HINDI URDU	RUSSIAN
CZECH	ITALIAN	SPANISH
FRENCH	JAPANESE	THAI
GERMAN	PORTUGUESE	TURKISH

For a catalogue please contact:
BBC Books,   Tel: 01624 675137
Book Service by Post,   Fax: 01624 670923
PO Box 29,
Douglas,
Isle of Man,
IM99 1BQ

BBC books are available at all good bookshops or direct from the
publishers as above.

Cover designed by Peter Bridgewater and Annie Moss

Published by BBC Books
A Division of BBC Worldwide Ltd
Woodlands, 80 Wood Lane, London W12 0TT

First published 1993
This edition published in 1995
Reprinted 1996

© Bengisu Rona 1993

ISBN 0 563 40000 5

Set in 8pt Monotype Times by Ace Filmsetting Ltd, Frome
Printed and bound in England by Clays Ltd, St Ives plc
Cover printed by Clays Ltd, St Ives plc

Contents

HOW TO USE THIS BOOK

Communicating in a foreign language doesn't have to be difficult – you can convey a lot with just a few words (plus a few gestures and a bit of mime). Just remember: keep it simple. Don't try to come out with long, grammatically perfect sentences when one or two words will get your meaning across.

Inside the back cover of this book is a list of all-purpose phrases. Some will help you to make contact – greetings, 'please' and 'thank you', 'yes' and 'no'. Some are to get people to help you understand what they're saying to you. And some are questions like 'do you have . . . ?' and 'where is . . . ?', to which you can add words from the Dictionary at the back of the book.

The book is divided into sections for different situations, such as Road Travel, Shopping, Health and so on. In each section you'll find
● Useful tips and information
● Words and phrases that you'll see on signs or in print
● Phrases you're likely to want to say
● Things that people may say to you.

Many of the phrases can be adapted by simply using another word from the Dictionary. For instance, take the question **Postane nerede?** (Where's the post office?). If you want to know where the police station is, just substitute **karakol** (police station) for **postane** (post office) to give **Karakol nerede?**

All the phrases have a simple pronunciation guide underneath based on English sounds – this is explained in Pronunciation (page 7).

If you want some guidance on how the Turkish language works, see Basic grammar (page 155).

There's a handy reference section (starts on page 170) which contains lists of days and months, countries and nationalities, general signs and notices that you'll see, conversion tables, national holidays, useful addresses and numbers.

The 5000-word Dictionary (page 191) comes in two sections: Turkish–English and English–Turkish.

A concise list of numbers is printed inside the front cover for easy reference, and right at the end of the book is an Emergencies section (which we hope you *won't* have to use).

Wherever possible, work out in advance what you want to say – if you're going shopping, for instance, write out a shopping list in Turkish. If you're buying travel tickets, work out how to say where you want to go, how many tickets you want, single or return, etc.

Practise saying things out loud – the cassette that goes with this book will help you to get used to the sounds of Turkish.

Above all – don't be shy! It'll be appreciated if you try to say a few words, even if it's only 'good morning' and 'goodbye' – and in fact those are the very sorts of phrases that are worth memorising, as you'll hear them and need to use them all the time.

If you'd like to learn more Turkish, BBC Books also publishes *Get by in Turkish*. BBC phrase books with pronunciation cassettes are also available for the following languages: Arabic, French, German, Greek, Italian, Portuguese and Spanish.

The author would welcome any suggestions or comments about this book, but in the meantime, have a good trip – **iyi yolculuklar!**

PRONUNCIATION

Turkish pronunciation is very regular: you can tell how a word is pronounced from the way it's written, once you know what sound each letter represents.

Some Turkish vowel sounds are quite different from sounds that exist in English – listen to the cassette to find out how they're pronounced.

Many Turkish consonants are pronounced in much the same way as in English. A pronunciation guide is given with the phrases in this book – the system is based on English sounds as described below.

Stress

Turkish words carry only a very light stress, generally on the last syllable, e.g. **güzel** (nice, beautiful), **rahat** (comfortable). The main exceptions to this are:

1 Most place names are stressed on the first syllable, e.g. **Ankara**, **İzmir**, **Erzurum** – except for **İstanbul**, which is stressed on the second syllable. Most adverbs are also stressed on the first syllable, e.g. **şimdi** (now), **sonra** (later), **yarın** (tomorrow).

2 Some verb endings are never stressed, even though they may be the last syllable in a word – in which case the stress is on the preceding syllable, e.g. **geliyor** (he is coming) **gelme** (don't come).

3 Question words like **nasıl** (how), **nerede** (where), **niçin** (why), etc. are stressed on the first syllable. They also have the strongest stress in the sentence.

On the whole, though, stresses are hardly noticeable when

words are strung together in phrases and sentences, so in this book they are not shown.

Vowels

	Approx. English equivalent	Shown in book as	Example	
a	between u in 'bus' and a in 'cat'	*a*	**at**	*at*
a+y	i in 'like'	*iy*	**ayak**	*iyak*
e	e in 'met'	*e*	**sepet**	*sepet*
i	between i in 'bit' and ee in 'feet'	*i*	**ilik**	*ilik*
ı	e in 'the cat'	*uh*	**ılık**	*uhluhk*
o	o in 'hot'	*o*	**ot**	*ot*
ö	or in 'word'	*ö*	**börek**	*börek*
u	between u in 'put' and oo in 'boot'	*u*	**uzun**	*uzun*
ü	between oo in 'too' and ew in 'new' (like French u in 'tu' or German ü in 'Düsseldorf')	*ew*	**üzüm**	*ewzewm*

Turkish vowels are generally short, except as described below. In the pronunciation guide, a long vowel is shown by a colon (:) placed after it.

1 If a vowel is followed by ğ, then it's pronounced long, and there's no 'g' sound, e.g.:
   bağ   *ba:* (vineyard)   **ağrı**   *a:ruh* (pain, ache)
   doğum   *do:um* (birth)   **iğne**   *i:ne* (needle)

2 Some words borrowed from other languages (especially Arabic and Persian) have kept their long vowels in Turkish, e.g.:
   lazım   *la:zuhm* (necessary)   **dahil**   *da:hil* (included)

Consonants

	Approx. English equivalent	Shown in book as	Example	
b	b in 'but'	*b*	**bak**	*bak*
c	j in 'jam'	*j*	**can**	*jan*
ç	ch in 'church'	*ch*	**çan**	*chan*
d	d in 'dog'	*d*	**dere**	*dere*
f	f in 'feet'	*f*	**efendim**	*efendim*
g	g in 'got'	*g*	**gece**	*geje*
ğ	not pronounced, but makes preceding vowel longer (see above under Vowels)	:	**dağ**	*da:*
h	h in 'hot'	*h*	**hangi**	*hangi*
j	s in 'measure'	*zh*	**ruj**	*ruzh*
k	k in 'kit'	*k*	**kan**	*kan*
l	l in 'lock'	*l*	**al**	*al*
m	m in 'mat'	*m*	**meze**	*meze*
n	n in 'not'	*n*	**niçin**	*nichin*
p	p in 'pack'	*p*	**ip**	*ip*
r	rolled as in Scottish accent	*r*	**arı**	*aruh*
s	s in 'set'	*s*	**sinema**	*sinema*
ş	sh in 'shoe'	*sh*	**şiş**	*shish*
t	t in 'tin'	*t*	**temiz**	*temiz*
v	v in 'vet'	*v*	**ve**	*ve*
y	y in 'yet'	*y*	**yeni**	*yeni*
z	z in 'zoo'	*z*	**zil**	*zil*

If there is a double consonant, both of them are pronounced.

THE TURKISH ALPHABET

There are 29 letters in the Turkish alphabet. They include all the letters of the English alphabet except **q**, **w** and **x**, plus six other letters: **ç**, **ğ**, **ş**, **ı**, **ö**, **ü**. In the alphabet, **ç**, **ğ**, **ş**, **ö** and **ü** come after **c**, **g**, **s**, **o** and **u** respectively. The letter **ı** (capital I, small letter **ı**, both written without a dot) comes before **İ/i** (both with a dot).

The names of the Turkish letters are given below in case you need to spell out a word. Punctuation is the same as in English. Proper nouns (names) take an apostrophe before an ending is added, e.g.

İstanbul'dan   from Istanbul
Ali'ye   to Ali

You may sometimes see a circumflex accent (^) over the vowel **a** or **ı**. This is found in only a few borrowed words and mostly shows that the vowel is long. The present tendency is not to use it in print.

Letter	Pronounced
A	*a*
B	*be*
C	*je*
Ç	*che*
D	*de*
E	*e*
F	*fe*
G	*ge*
Ğ yumuşak ğ	*yumushak ge*
H	*he*
I	*uh*

İ	*ee*
J	*zhe*
K	*ke*
L	*le*
M	*me*
N	*ne*
O	*o*
Ö	*ö*
P	*pe*
R	*re*
S	*se*
Ş	*she*
T	*te*
U	*oo*
Ü	*ew*
V	*ve*
Y	*ye*
Z	*ze*

GENERAL CONVERSATION

• The word **merhaba** is an informal greeting that means 'hello'. More formal greetings depend on the time of day: you can say **iyi günler** (good day) until early evening, and **iyi akşamlar** (good evening) after that. In the morning you can also say **günaydın** (good morning), but there's no phrase for 'good afternoon'.

In rural areas in particular you will hear the traditional religious greeting **Selamünaleykum** (Peace be with you). The reply is **Aleykumselam** (Peace be with you too).

When saying 'goodbye' in Turkish the person leaving says **Allahaısmarladık** (literally 'I leave you in God's care') and the person staying behind says **güle güle** (literally 'may you go smiling', meaning happily). You can also use **iyi günler** or **iyi akşamlar** to say goodbye, with or without **Allahaısmarladık** or **güle güle**.

• In Turkey people usually shake hands when they meet and when they part. Very close friends or family kiss each other on both cheeks.

• There are two different words for 'you' in Turkish: **sen** (informal) and **siz** (formal), with different endings on the verbs. We've used the formal 'you' in this book, because as a tourist in Turkey you will probably find yourself more in formal situations.

• When introducing people or addressing those with whom you are on formal terms, you put **Bey** (for men) and **Hanım** (for women) after their first names, e.g. **Ahmet Bey** or **Ayşe Hanım**. To be more formal, you put **Sayın** (both for men and for women) before the surname, e.g. **Sayın Sevgen, Sayın**

Arıç. Alternatively you can put **Bay** (for men) or **Bayan** (for women) before the surnames, e.g. **Bay Sevgen** or **Bayan Arıç**, which is like saying Mr Sevgen or Ms Arıç.

Greetings

Hello
Merhaba
merhaba

Good day
İyi günler
i-yi gewnler

Good morning
Günaydın
gewniyduhn

Good evening
İyi akşamlar
i-yi akshamlar

Goodnight
İyi geceler
i-yi gejeler

Goodbye
Allahaısmarladık (if you're leaving)
ala:smalduhk

Goodbye
Güle güle (if you're staying behind)
gewle gewle

See you later
Görüşmek üzere
görewshmek ewzere

How are you?
Nasılsınız?
nasuhlsuhnuhz

Fine, thanks
İyiyim, teşekkür ederim
i-yi-yim, teshekkewr ederim

And you?
Ya siz?
ya siz

Introductions

My name is ...
İsmim ...
ismim ...

(This is) Mr Brown
Bay Brown
biy brown

(This is) Mrs Clark
Bayan Clark
biyan clark

(This) is my boyfriend
Erkek arkadaşım
erkek arkadashuhm

(This is) my wife/husband
Eşim
eshim

(This is) my fiancée/fiancé
Nişanlım
nishanluhm

(This is) my daughter/son
Kızım/Oğlum
kuhzuhm/o:lum

Pleased to meet you
Memnun oldum
memnun oldum

(This is) my girlfriend
Kızarkadaşım
kuhz arkadashuhm

Talking about yourself and your family

(See Countries and nationalities, page 176)

14

I am English/British
Ben İngilizim
ben ingilizim

We live in Birmingham
Birmingham'da oturuyoruz
birminghamda oturuyoruz

I am Scottish
Ben İskoçyalıyım
ben iskochyaluhyuhm

I am a student
Ben öğrenciyim
ben ö:renjiyim

I am Irish
Ben İrlandalıyım
ben irlandaluhyuhm

I am a teacher
Ben öğretmenim
ben ö:retmenim

I am Welsh
Ben Galliyim
ben galliyim

I work ...
... çalışıyorum
... chaluhshuhyorum

I live in London
Londra'da oturuyorum
londrada oturuyorum

I work in an office/in a factory
Büroda/fabrikada çalışıyorum
bewroda/fabrikada chaluhshuhyorum

I work for a computer company
Bir kompüter şirketinde çalışıyorum
bir kompewter shirketinde chaluhshuhyorum

I am unemployed
İşsizim
ishsizim

I am single
Bekarım
bekaruhm

I am married
Evliyim
evli-yim

I am separated
Eşimden ayrıldım
eshimden iyruhlduhm

I am divorced
Eşimden boşandım
eshimden boshanduhm

I am a widow/widower
Dulum
dulum

I have a son/a daughter
Bir oğlum/kızım var
bir o:lum/kuhzuhm var

I have three children
Üç çocuğum var
ewch choju:um var

I don't have any children
Çocuğum yok
choju:um yok

I have one brother
Bir erkek kardeşim var
bir erkek kardeshim var

I have three sisters
Üç kızkardeşim var
ewch kuhzkardeshim var

I'm here with my husband/wife
Ben burada eşimleyim
ben burada eshimleyim

I'm here with my family
Ben burada ailemleyim
ben burada a:ilemleyim

I'm here on holiday
Burada tatildeyim
burada ta:tildeyim

I'm here on business
İş için buradayım
ish ichin buradayuhm

I speak very little Turkish
Çok az Türkçe biliyorum
chok az tewrkche biliyorum

My husband/wife is ...
Eşim ...
eshim ...

My husband/wife works in a hospital
Eşim bir hastanede çalışıyor
eshim bir hastanede chaluhshuhyor

My husband/wife works ...
Eşim ... çalışıyor
eshim ...chaluhshuhyor

My son is five years old
Oğlum beş yaşında
o:lum besh yashuhnda

My husband is a bus-driver
Eşim otobüs şoförü
eshim otobews shoförew

My daughter is eight years old
Kızım sekiz yaşında
kuzzuhm sekiz yashuhnda

My wife is an accountant
Eşim hesap uzmanı
eshim hesap uzmanuh

You may hear

İsminiz ne?
isminiz ne
What is your name?

Ne okuyorsunuz?
ne okuyorsunuz
What do you study?

Nerelisiniz?
nerelisiniz
Where are you from?

Evli misiniz?
evli misiniz
Are you married?

Ne yapıyorsunuz?
ne yapuhyorsunuz
What do you do?

Çocuklarınız var mı?
chojuklaruhnuhz varmuh
Do you have children?

Ne iş yapıyorsunuz?
ne ish yapuhyorsunuz
What job do you do?

Kaç yaşındalar?
kach yashuhndalar
How old are they?

Öğrenci misiniz?
ö:renji misiniz
Are you a student?

Kaç yaşında?
kach yashuhnda
How old is he/she?

Çok güzel
chok gewzel
He/she is very nice/beautiful

Kardeşleriniz var mı?
kardeshleriniz varmuh
Do you have any brothers and sisters?

Bu eşiniz mi?
bu eshinizmi
Is this your husband/wife?

Bu nişanlınız mı?
bu nishanluhnuhzmuh
Is this your fiancé/fiancée?

Bu erkek arkadaşınız mı?
bu erkek arkadashuhnuhz muh
Is this your boyfriend?

Bu kız arkadaşınız mı?
bu kuhz arkadashuhnuhz muh
Is this your girlfriend?

Bu arkadaşınız mı?
bu arkadashuhnuhz muh
Is this your friend?

Nereye gidiyorsunuz?
nereye gidiyorsunuz
Where are you going?

Nerede kalıyorsunuz?
nerede kaluhyorsunuz
Where are you staying?

Nerede oturuyorsunuz?
nerede oturuyorsunuz
Where do you live?

Talking about Turkey and your own country

I like Turkey (very much)
Türkiye'yi (çok) seviyorum
tewrkiyeyi (chok) seviyorum

Turkey is very beautiful
Türkiye çok güzel
tewrkiye chok gewzel

This is the first time I've been to Turkey
Türkiye'ye ilk defa geliyorum
tewrkiyeye ilk defa geliyorum

I come to Turkey often
Türkiye'ye sık sık geliyorum
tewrkiyeye suhk suhk geliyorum

Are you from here?
Siz buralı mısınız?
siz buraluh muhsuhnuhz

Have you ever been to England?
İngiltere'ye hiç gittiniz mi?
ingiltereye hich gittinizmi

... to Scotland/ ... to Ireland/ ... to Wales
İskoçya'ya .../İrlanda'ya .../ Galler'e ...
iskochya-ya .../irlanda-ya .../ gallere ...

You may hear

Türkiye'yi seviyor musunuz?
tewrkiyeyi seviyor musunuz
Do you like Turkey?

Türkiye'ye ilk defa mı geliyorsunuz?
tewrkiyeye ilk defa:muh geliyorsunuz
Is this your first time in Turkey?

Burada ne kadar kalacaksınız?
burada ne kadar kalajaksuhnuhz
How long are you here for?

Türkçeniz çok iyi
tewrkcheniz chok iyi
Your Turkish is very good

Likes and dislikes

I like/love ...
... seviyorum
... seviyorum

I like swimming
Yüzmeyi seviyorum
yewzmeyi seviyorum

I like dancing
Dansı seviyorum
dansuh seviyorum

I like it
Beğendim
be:endim

I don't like ...
... sevmiyorum
... sevmiyorum

I don't like beer
Bira sevmiyorum
bira sevmiyorum

I don't like playing tennis
Tenis oynamayı sevmiyorum
tenis oynamayuh sevmiyorum

I don't like it
Beğenmedim
be:enmedim

Do you like ...?
... sever misiniz?
... sever misiniz

Do you like ice-cream?
Dondurma sever misiniz?
dondurma sever misiniz

Do you like it?
Beğendiniz mi?
be:endinizmi

Did you like it?
Beğendiniz mi?
be:endinizmi

Talking to a child

What's your name?
İsmin ne?
ismin ne

How old are you?
Kaç yaşındasın?
kach yashuhndasuhn

Do you have any brothers
  and sisters?
Kardeşlerin var mı?
kardeshlerin varmuh

Invitations and replies

Would you like ...?
... ister misiniz?
... istermisiniz

Would you like some tea?
Çay ister misiniz?
chiy istermisiniz

Would you like a drink?
  (alcoholic)
İçki ister misiniz?
ichki istermisiniz

Yes, please
Evet, lütfen
evet lewtfen

No, thank you
Hayır, teşekkür ederim
hiyuhr teshekkewr ederim

I'd like that
Çok isterim
chok isterim

That would be nice
İyi olur
iyi olur

Please leave me alone
Lütfen rahatsız etmeyin
lewtfen rahatsuhz etmeyin

You may hear

... ister misiniz?
... ister misiniz
Would you like ... ?

Çay/kahve ister misiniz?
chiy/kahve ister misiniz
Would you like some tea/
  coffee?

İçki ister misiniz?
ichki ister misiniz
Would you like a drink?
  (alcoholic)

Bir şey yemek ister misiniz?
bir shey yemek ister misiniz
Would you like to eat
  something?

Bu gece ne yapıyorsunuz?
bu geje ne yapuhyorsunuz
What are you doing tonight?

... gitmek/gelmek ister misiniz?
... gitmek/gelmek ister misiniz
Would you like to go/
come ...?

Diskoya gitmek ister misiniz?
diskoya gitmek ister misiniz
Would you like to go to
the disco?

**Sinemaya gitmek ister
misiniz?**
sinemaya gitmek ister misiniz
Would you like to go to the
cinema?

Yemeğe gelmek ister misiniz?
yeme:e gelmek ister misiniz
Would you like to come to
dinner?

Dans etmek ister misiniz?
Dans etmek ister misiniz?
Would you like to dance?

Saat kaçta buluşalım?
saat kachta bulushaluhm
What time shall we meet?

Nerede buluşalım?
nerede bulushaluhm
Where shall we meet?

Kibritiniz var mı?
kibritiniz varmuh
Have you got a match?

Good wishes and exclamations

Congratulations!
Tebrikler!
tebrikler

Happy birthday!
Doğum gününüz kutlu olsun!
*do:um gewnewnewz kutlu
olsun*

Merry Christmas!
Mutlu Noeller!
mutlu noeller

Happy New Year!
Yeni yılınız kutlu olsun!
yeni yuhluhnuhz kutlu olsun

Happy Bayram!
Bayramınız kutlu olsun!
bayramuhnuhz kutlu olsun
(**Bayram** refers to the two
major Moslem festivals;
see page 186)

Good luck!
İyi şanslar!
i-yi shanslar

Enjoy yourself!
İyi eğlenceler!
i-yi e:lenjeler

Have a good journey!
İyi yolculuklar!
i-yi yoljuluklar

Cheers!
Şerefe!
sherefe

Enjoy your meal!
Afiyet olsun!
a:fi-yet olsun

Bless you! (*when someone sneezes*)
Çok yaşa! (literally 'live long')
chok yasha

I hope so!
İnşallah! (literally 'God willing')
inshallah

What a pity!
Yazık!
yazuhk

Talking about the weather

The weather's very good
Hava çok güzel
hava chok gewzel

The weather's very bad
Hava çok kötü
hava chok kötew

It's a lovely day
Çok güzel bir gün
chok gewzel bir gün

It's hot
Hava sıcak
hava suhjak

It's cold
Hava soğuk
hava so:uk

Phew, it's hot!
Çok sıcak!
chok suhjak

I like the heat
Sıcağı seviyorum
suhja:uh seviyorum

I don't like the heat
Sıcağı sevmiyorum
suhja:uh sevmiyorum

ARRIVING IN THE COUNTRY

● Visa requirements can vary depending on your nationality, but British citizens can pay (cash, in sterling) for a visa at the port of entry when they arrive.

● Passport control and Customs are quite straightforward. Duty-free allowances are generous and there are duty-free shops in the international arrivals section of major airports.

You may see

Açık	Open
Çekiniz	Pull
Çıkış	Exit
Giriş	Entry
Girmek yasaktır	Entry prohibited
Gümrük	Customs
Hoş geldiniz	Welcome
İtiniz	Push
Kapalı	Closed
Polis	Police
Sigara içilmez	No smoking
Taksi	Taxi

You may want to say

I've come here for a holiday
Tatil için geldim
ta:til ichin geldim

I've come here on business
İş için geldim
ish ichin geldim

It's a joint passport
Bu bir aile pasaportu
bu bir a:ile pasaportu

I have something to declare
Gümrüğe tabi eşyam var
gewmrew:e ta:bi: eshyam var

I have this
Bende bu var
bende bu var

I have two bottles of whisky
İki şişe viskim var
iki shishe viskim var

I have two cartons of
  cigarettes
İki karton sigaram var
iki karton sigaram var

I have a receipt for this
Bunun makbuzu bende var
bunun makbuzu bende var

You may hear

Pasaportunuz lütfen
pasaportunuz lewtfen
Your passport, please

Türkiye'ye niçin geldiniz?
tewrkiyeye nichin geldiniz
What's the purpose of your
  visit?

**İş için mi geldiniz, tatil için
mi?**
*ish ichinmi geldiniz tatil
  ichinmi*
Are you here on business
  or holiday?

Turist misiniz?
turist misiniz
Are you a tourist?

**Türkiye'de ne kadar
  kalacaksınız?**
*tewrkiyede ne kadar
  kalajaksuhnuhz*
How long are you staying
  in Turkey?

Hangi bavul sizin?
hangi bavul sizin
Which suitcase is yours?

Hangisi sizin?
hangisi sizin
Which is yours?

Bu bavulu/çantayı açın lütfen
*bu bavulu/chantiyuh achuhn
  lewtfen*
Please open this suitcase/bag

Hepsi sizin mi?
hepsi sizinmi
Is it all yours?

Lütfen bagajı açın
lewtfen bagazhuh achuhn
Please open the boot

Arabayı aramamız lazım
arabiyuh aramamuhz la:zuhm
We have to search the car

Başka eşyanız var mı?
bashka eshyanuhz varmuh
Do you have any other luggage?

Gümrük ödemeniz lazım
gewmrewk ödemeniz la:zuhm
You have to pay duty

Benimle gelin lütfen
benimle gelin lewtfen
Please come with me

Beni izleyin
beni izleyin
Follow me

DIRECTIONS

● Some general information about Turkey and basic maps are available from the Turkish Tourist Office in London (address on page 187). Guidebooks and road maps are obtainable in bookshops. Once in Turkey most local tourist offices can provide town plans and regional maps.

● When you need to ask something, the easiest way to attract attention is to say **affedersiniz** (excuse me) followed by your question.

● To ask where something is, say the word for what you're looking for followed by **nerede** (where?), e.g. **Postane nerede?** (Where is the post office?); **Giriş nerede?** (Where is the entrance?).

● If you're looking for a particular address, have it written down. In Turkey, addresses are written with the street name first and the number afterwards, e.g. **Gençlik Caddesi, 14**. An address for an office or a flat may also show the name of the apartment block and the number of the flat, e.g. **Yazanlar Sokak, Çam apt. 8/3**, where 8 is the building number and 3 is the number of the flat.

● When you're being given directions, listen out for the important bits such as whether to turn right or left, and try to repeat each bit to make sure you've understood it correctly. You can always ask the person to say it again more slowly: **Bir daha lütfen** (Once more, please); **Daha yavaş** (More slowly).

You may see

Bulvar	Boulevard
Cadde	Road
Cami	Mosque
Centrum	Town centre
Çıkmaz sokak	Dead-end street, cul-de-sac
Kale	Castle/fortress
Kilise	Church
Köprü	Bridge
Köşk	Mansion
Mağara	Cave
Meydan	Square
Müze	Museum
Saray	Palace
Sokak	Street
Şehir merkezi	City centre
Yeraltı geçidi	Subway

You may want to say

Excuse me please
Affedersiniz
affedersiniz

Again
Tekrar
tekrar

What did you say?
Efendim?
efendim

I am lost
Kayboldum
kiyboldum

Once more please
Bir daha lütfen
bir daha lewtfen

Where are we?
Neredeyiz?
neredeyiz

More slowly
Daha yavaş
daha yavash

Where does this street/road lead to?
Bu sokak/cadde nereye gider?
bu sokak/jadde nereye gider

Is this the road to Bursa?
Bursa yolu bu mu?
bursa yolu bumu

The road to İznik, please?
İznik yolu lütfen?
iznik yolu lewtfen

Could you show me on the map?
Haritada gösterir misiniz?
haritada gösterirmisiniz

How do I get to ...?
... nasıl giderim?
... nasuhl giderim

Excuse me please, how do I get to the station?
Affedersiniz, istasyona nasıl giderim?
affedersiniz istasyona nasuhl giderim

How do I get to the town centre?
Şehir merkezine nasıl giderim?
shehir merkezine nasuhl giderim

How do I get to the airport?
Havaalanına nasıl giderim?
havaalanuhna nasuhl giderim

How do I get to the beach?
Plaja nasıl giderim?
plazha nasuhl giderim

Where is/are ...?
... nerede?
... nerede

Where is this? (*if you've got an address written down*)
Burası nerede?
burasuh nerede

Where is the tourist office/ information?
Turizm bürosu/danışma nerede?
turizm bewrosu/danuhshma nerede

Where is the post office?
Postane nerede?
posta:ne nerede

Where is this room?
Bu oda nerede?
bu oda nerede

Where is the shop?
Dükkan nerede?
dewkkan nerede

Where is the toilet?
Tuvalet nerede?
tuvalet nerede

Is it far?
Uzak mı?
uzakmuh

Can I get there on foot?
Yürüyerek gidebilir miyim?
yewrewyerek gidebilir mi-yim

Is the airport far away?
Havaalanı uzak mı?
havaalanuh uzakmuh

Can I get there by car?
Arabayla gidebilir miyim?
arabiyla gidebilir mi-yim

How many kilometres away?
Kaç kilometre uzakta?
kach kilometre uzakta

Is/are there ...?
... var mı?
... varmuh

How long does it take (on foot/by car)?
(Yürüyerek/arabayla) ne kadar sürer?
(yewrewyerek/arabiyla) ne kadar sewrer

Is there a bank around here?
Buralarda banka var mı?
buralarda banka varmuh

Is there a supermarket here?
Burada süpermarket var mı?
burada sewpermarket varmuh

Is there a bus/train?
Otobüs/tren var mı?
otobews/tren varmuh

28

You may hear

Yanlış yaptınız
yanluhsh yaptuhnuhz
You've made a mistake

Orada/şurada
orada/shurada
There

Buradayız
buradiyuhz
We are here

Bu tarafta
bu tarafta
This way

Burada
burada
Here

O tarafta
o tarafta
That way/on that side

Sağa
sa:a
To the right

Sola
sola
To the left

Düz/doğru gidin
dewz/do:ru gidin
Go straight on

Birinci sokak
birinji sokak
The first street/turning

İkinci sokak
ikinji sokak
The second street/turning

Üçüncü sokak
ewchewnjew sokak
The third street

Sağ tarafta
sa: tarafta
On the right-hand side

Sol tarafta
sol tarafta
On the left-hand side

Yolun/sokağın sonunda
yolun/soka:uhn sonunda
At the end of the road/street

Meydanın öbür tarafında
meydanuhn öbewr tarafuhnda
On the other side of the
square

Köşede
köshede
On the corner

Aşağıda
asha:uhda
Down there/downstairs

Yukarıda
yukaruhda
Up there/upstairs

Altta
altta
Under

Üstte
ewstte
Over/on top

**Işıklardan/trafik
  ışıklarından önce**
*uhshuhklardan/trafik
  uhshuhklaruhndan önje*
Before the lights/traffic lights

**Camiden sonra/Camiyi
  geçince**
*ja:miden sonra/ja:mi-yi
  gechinje*
After/past the mosque

... karşısında
... karshuhsuhnda
Opposite ...

... arkasında
... arkasuhnda
Behind ...

29

... yanında
... yanuhnda
Next to/beside ...

Yakında
yakuhnda
Nearby/close

... yakınında
... yakuhnuhnda
Near to/close to ...

... gelince
... gelinje
When you get to ...

Camiye doğru
ja:miye do:ru
Towards the mosque

Köşeye kadar
kösheye kadar
As far as the corner

Işıklara/trafik ışıklarına kadar
uhshuhklara/trafik uhshuhklaruhna kadar
As far as the lights/traffic lights

Uzak değil
uzak de:il
It's not far away

Biraz/çok uzak
biraz/chok uzak
Quite/very far

Çok yakın
chok yakuhn
Very near

Beş dakika ötede/uzakta
besh dakika ötede/uzakta
It's five minutes away

Yirmi kilometre ötede/uzakta
yirmi kilometre ötede/uzakta
It's twenty kilometres away

On kilometre ilerde
on kilometre ilerde
It's ten kilometres ahead

Otobüsle/trenle gitmeniz lazım
otobüsle/trenle gitmeniz la:zuhm
You have to go by bus/train

Üçüncü katta
ewchewnjew katta
It's on the third floor

Birinci/ikinci kat
birinji/ikinji kat
The first/second floor

Asansöre binin
asansöre binin
Take the lift

... gidin
... gidin
Go ...

Devam edin
deva:m edin
Carry on/go on

Aşağı inin
asha:uh inin
Go down

Yukarı çıkın
yukaruh chuhkuhn
Go up

... dönün
dönewn
Turn ...

Karşıya geçin
karshuhya gechin
Cross over

Geri dönün
geri dönewn
Go/turn back

ROAD TRAVEL

• You drive on the right in Turkey. Seatbelts are compulsory in the front seats. For further information on driving, consult the Turkish motoring organisation **Türkiye Turing ve Otomobil Kurumu** or the Tourist Office (addresses, page 187).

• Petrol stations are not usually self-service, so you will need to ask for what you want. Opening hours vary, but many stay open until midnight, and in large cities and on motorways some offer a 24-hour service. Unleaded petrol is available at some petrol stations.

• Large cities suffer from traffic congestion, and parking is often a problem. Car parks usually have an attendant, and there are some multi-storey car parks. Major international hotels in Istanbul and Ankara have underground car parks. Beware of No Parking signs – yellow lines are not used in Turkey. If you park illegally, your car may be clamped or towed away.

• Roads between the major cities in Turkey are mostly in good condition but are also quite busy. Road markings are not very good and it is not advisable to drive at night as vehicles, especially stationary ones, are often poorly lit. Roads in mountainous areas in eastern Turkey often have poor surfaces, as do secondary roads in many parts of the country. There are a few toll-roads of motorway standard between Ankara and Istanbul and on other major routes.

• Car hire can be arranged in the UK and Ireland with the large international firms, which have offices in major cities and towns and at the principal airports in Turkey. There are also some local companies.

You may see

Ağır vasıta	Heavy goods vehicle
Ambulans	Ambulance
Araba tamirhanesi	Car repair shop
Araç çıkabilir	Vehicles exiting
Askeri araç	Military vehicle
Askeri bölge	Military zone
Azami hız	Maximum speed
Benzin istasyonu	Petrol station
Dar geçit	Narrow passage
Demiryolu geçidi	Level crossing
Dikkat	Caution/Attention
Dur	Stop
Ekspres yol	Motorway
Farlarınızı yakınız	Switch on your headlights
Farlarınızı kapatınız	Switch off your headlights
Geçmek yasaktır	Do not cross/proceed
Giriş	Entrance
Girişi kapatmayın	Do not block entrance
Girmek yasaktır	Entry prohibited
İlk yardım	First aid
Kamyon çıkabilir	Lorries exiting
Kavşak	Junction
Kemerlerinizi bağlayınız	Fasten your seatbelts
Kiralık araba	Car hire
Köprü	Bridge
Mecburi istikamet	Compulsory route
Okul	School
Otopark	Car park
Oto tamircisi	Car mechanic
Otoyol	Motorway
Paralı geçiş	Toll
Park etmek yasaktır	Parking prohibited
Park yapılmaz	No parking

Polis	Police
Sis	Fog
Sollamak yasaktır	No overtaking
Taksi	Taxi
Taşıt giremez	No entry to vehicles
Tamirhane	Garage
TCDD	Turkish Railways
Tehlike	Danger
Tehlikeli madde	Dangerous substances
Tehlikeli virajlar	Dangerous bends
Trafik ışıkları	Traffic lights
Tek yön	One way
Uzun araç	Long vehicle
Yangın	Fire
Yasak	Forbidden
Yavaş	Slow
Yaya geçidi	Pedestrian crossing
Yerel trafik	Local traffic
Yol tamiratı	Road works
Yol ver	Give way

You may want to say

Petrol

Is there a petrol station
  near here?
**Yakında benzin istasyonu
  var mı?**
*yakuhnda benzin istasyonu
  varmuh*

4-star
Süper
sewper

2-star
Normal
normal

Unleaded petrol
Kurşunsuz benzin
kurshunsuz benzin

Diesel
Dizel
dizel

20 litres of 4-star, please
Yirmi litre süper, lütfen
yirmi litre sewper lewtfen

50,000 liras' worth of
unleaded petrol
**Elli bin liralık kurşunsuz
benzin**
*elli bin liraluhk kurshunsuz
benzin*

Fill it up with 4-star/2-star
Süper/Normal doldurun
sewper/normal doldurun

A can of oil
Bir teneke yağ
bir teneke ya:

Water, please
Su, lütfen
su lewtfen

Could you change the tyre?
Lastiği değiştirir misiniz?
lasti:i de:ishtirir misiniz

Could you check the tyre
pressures?
**Lastiklerin havasını kontrol
eder misiniz?**
*lastiklerin havasuhnuh
kontrol eder misiniz*

Could you clean the
windscreen?
Öncamı yıkar mısınız?
önjamuh yuhkar muhsuhnuhz

Where is the air line?
Hava pompası nerede?
hava pompasuh nerede

How does the car-wash work?
**Otomatik yıkama nasıl
çalışıyor?**
*otomatik yuhkama nasuhl
chaluhshuhyor*

How much is it?
Kaç para?
kach para

Parking

Where can I park?
Nerede park edebilirim?
nerede park edebilirim

Can I park here?
Burada park edebilir miyim?
burada park edebilirmiyim

How long can I park here?
**Burada kaç saat park
edebilirim?**
*burada kach saat park
edebilirim*

How much is it per hour?
Saati kaça?
saati kacha

Hiring a car

(See Days, months, dates, page 170)

I want to hire a car
Bir araba kiralamak istiyorum
bir araba kiralamak istiyorum

A small car, please
Küçük bir araba lütfen
kewchewk bir araba lewtfen

A medium-sized car, please
Orta boy bir araba lütfen
orta boy bir araba lewtfen

A large car, please
Büyük bir araba lütfen
bewyewk bir araba lewtfen

An automatic car, please
Otomatik vitesli bir araba lütfen
otomatik vitesli bir araba lewtfen

For three days
Üç gün için
ewch gewn ichin

For a week
Bir hafta için
bir hafta ichin

For two weeks
İki hafta için
iki hafta ichin

From Monday to Friday
Pazartesi'den Cuma'ya kadar
pazartesiden juma:ya kadar

From 10th September to 17th September
On Eylül'den on yedi Eylül'e kadar
on eylewlden on yedi eylewle kadar

How much is it?
Kaç para?
kach para

Per day/week
Bir günlük/haftalık
bir gewnlewk/haftaluhk

Per kilometre
Kilometre başına
kilometre bashuhna

Is mileage/kilometrage included?
Kilometraj dahil mi?
kilometrazh da:hilmi

Is petrol included?
Benzin dahil mi?
benzin da:hilmi

Is insurance included?
Sigorta dahil mi?
sigorta da:hilmi

Comprehensive insurance
Tam sigorta
tam sigorta

My husband/wife will be driving too
Eşim de arabayı kullanacak
eshimde arabayuh kullanajak

Do you take credit cards?
Kredi kartı kabul ediyor musunuz?
kredi kartuh kabul ediyor-musunuz

Do you take travellers' cheques?
Seyahat çeki kabul ediyor musunuz?
seyahat cheki kabul ediyor-musunuz

Can I leave the car in Kuşadası?
Arabayı Kuşadasında bırakabilir miyim?
arabiyuh kushadasuhnda buhrakabilir mi-yim

Can I leave the car at the airport?
Arabayı havaalanında bırakabilir miyim?
arabiyuh havaalanuhnda buhrakabilir mi-yim

How does it work?
Nasıl çalışıyor?
nasuhl chaluhshuhyor

Breakdowns and repairs

(See Car and bicycle parts, page 41)

My car has broken down
Arabam bozuldu
arabam bozuldu

Is there a garage around here?
**Yakında bir tamirhane var
mı?**
*yakuhnda bir ta:mirha:ne
varmuh*

Could you telephone a
garage?
**Bir tamirhaneye telefon
eder misiniz?**
*bir ta:mirha:neye telefon
eder misiniz*

Could you send a mechanic?
Bir tamirci gönderir misiniz?
bir ta:mirji gönderir misiniz

Could you tow the car to a
garage?
**Arabayı bir tamirhaneye
çeker misiniz?**
*arabayuh bir ta:mirha:neye
cheker misiniz*

Do you do repairs?
Tamir yapıyor musunuz?
ta:mir yapuhyor musunuz

I don't know what's wrong
Ne bozuk bilmiyorum
ne bozuk bilmiyorum

I think ...
... sanıyorum
... sanuhyorum

It's the clutch
Debriyaj
debriyazh

It's the radiator
Radyatör
radyatör

It's the brakes
Frenler
frenler

The car won't start
Araba çalışmıyor
araba chaluhshmuhyor

The battery is flat
Akü boşalmış
akew boshalmuhsh

The engine is overheating
Motor ısınıyor
motor uhsuhnuhyor

It's losing water/oil
Su/Yağ akıtıyor
su/ya: akuhtuhyor

I've had a puncture
Lastik patladı
lastik patladuh

I've run out of petrol
Benzin bitti
benzin bitti

The ... doesn't work
... çalışmıyor
... chaluhshmuhyor

I need a ...
... lazım
... la:zuhm

Is it serious?
Önemli mi?
önemlimi

Could you repair it (today)?
(Bugün) tamir edebilir misiniz?
*(bugewn) ta:mir edebilir
misiniz*

When will it be ready?
Ne zaman hazır olur?
ne zaman hazuhr olur

How much will it cost?
Kaç para tutar?
kach para tutar

You may hear

Petrol

Ne istiyorsunuz?
ne istiyorsunuz
What would you like?

Ne kadar istiyorsunuz?
ne kadar istiyorsunuz
How much do you want?

Anahtar lütfen
anahtar lewtfen
The key, please

Parking

Burada park edemezsiniz
burada park edemezsiniz
You can't park here

Saati beş bin lira
saati besh bin lira
It's five thousand liras an
hour

Parasız
parasuhz
It's free

Orada bir otopark var
orada bir otopark var
There's a car park over there

Hiring a car

Nasıl bir araba istiyorsunuz?
nasuhl bir araba istiyorsunuz
What kind of car do you want?

Kaç gün için?
kach gewn ichin
For how many days?

(Fiyatı) iki yüz elli bin lira
(fiyatuh) iki yewz elli bin lira
(The price is) 250 thousand liras

Bir günlük
bir gewnlewk
Per day

Haftalık
haftaluhk
Per week

Kim kullanacak?
kim kullanajak
Who's driving?

Ehliyetiniz lütfen
ehliyetiniz lewtfen
Your driving licence please

Adresiniz nedir?
adresiniz nedir
What is your address?

Buyurun anahtarlar
buyurun anahtarlar
Here are the keys

Arabayı geri getirirken benzin deposunu doldurun lütfen
arabiyuh geri getirirken benzin deposunu doldurun lewtfen
Please return the car with a full tank

Arabayı saat altıdan önce getirin lütfen
arabiyuh saat altuhdan önje getirin lewtfen
Please bring the car back before six

Breakdowns and repairs

Nesi var?
nesi var
What's wrong with it?

Kaputu açar mısınız?
kaputu achar muhsuhnuhz
Could you open the bonnet?

Gerekli parça yok
gerekli parcha yok
I don't have the necessary
parts

Parça ısmarlamak lazım
parcha uhsmarlamak la:zuhm
I'll have to order the parts

Gelecek Salı'ya hazır olur
gelejek saluhya hazuhr olur
It'll be ready by next Tuesday

Yüz seksen bin lira tutar
yewz seksen bin lira tutar
It'll cost 180 thousand liras

Car and bicycle parts

Accelerator	**Gaz pedalı**	*gaz pedaluh*
Air filter	**Hava filtresi**	*hava filtresi*
Alternator	**Alternatör**	*alternatör*
Battery	**Akü**	*akew*
Bonnet	**Kaput**	*kaput*
Brake cable	**Fren kablosu**	*fren kablosu*
Brake fluid	**Fren yağı**	*fren ya:uh*
Brakes (front/rear)	**Frenler (ön/arka)**	*frenler (ön/arka)*
Carburettor	**Karbüratör**	*karbewratör*
Chain	**Zincir**	*zinjir*
Choke	**Jikle**	*zhikle*
Clutch	**Debriyaj**	*debri-yazh*
Cooling system	**Soğutma sistemi**	*so:utma sistemi*
Disc brakes	**Disk frenler**	*disk frenler*
Distributor	**Distribütör**	*distribewtör*
Electrical system	**Elektrik sistemi**	*elektrik sistemi*
Engine	**Motor**	*motor*
Exhaust pipe	**Egsoz borusu**	*egsoz borusu*
Fanbelt	**Vantilatör kayışı**	*vantilatör kayuhshu*
Fuel gauge	**Benzin göstergesi**	*benzin göstergesi*
Fuel pump	**Benzin pompası**	*benzin pompasuh*
Fuse/fuses	**Sigorta**	*sigorta*
Gearbox	**Vites kutusu**	*vites kutusu*
Gear lever	**Vites kolu**	*vites kolu*

Handbrake	**El freni**	*el freni*
Handlebars	**Gidon**	*gidon*
Headlights	**Farlar**	*farlar*
Heater	**Kalorifer**	*kalorifer*
Horn	**Klakson**	*klakson*
Ignition	**Kontak**	*kontak*
Ignition key	**Kontak anahtarı**	*kontak anahtaruh*
Indicator	**Sinyal kolu**	*sinyal kolu*
Indicator light	**Sinyal lambası**	*sinyal lambasuh*
Lights (front/rear)	**Işıklar (ön/arka)**	*uhshuhklar(ön/arka)*
Lock	**Kilit**	*kilit*
Oil filter	**Yağ filtresi**	*ya: filtresi*
Oil gauge	**Yağ göstergesi**	*ya: göstergesi*
Pedal	**Pedal**	*pedal*
Points	**Platin**	*platin*
Pump	**Pompa**	*pompa*
Radiator	**Radyatör**	*radyatör*
Radiator hose (top/bottom)	**Radyatör hortumu (üst/alt)**	*radyatör hortumu (ewst/alt)*
Reversing lights	**Geri gidiş lambaları**	*gerigidish lambalaruh*
Saddle	**Sele**	*sele*
Silencer	**Susturucu**	*susturuju*
Spare tyre	**Yedek lastik**	*yedek lastik*
Spark plugs	**Buji**	*buzhi*
Speedometer	**Hız göstergesi**	*huhz göstergesi*
Steering wheel	**Direksiyon**	*direksiyon*
Tyre (front/rear)	**Lastik (ön/arka)**	*lastik (ön/arka)*
Valve	**Supap**	*supap*
Warning light	**İkaz lambası**	*i:kaz lambasuh*
Wheel (front/rear)	**Tekerlek (ön/arka)**	*tekerlek (ön/arka)*
Window	**Cam**	*jam*
Windscreen	**Ön cam**	*ön jam*
Windscreen washer	**Cam yıkayıcısı**	*jam yuhkayuhjuhsuh*
Windscreen wiper	**Silecek**	*silejek*

TAXIS

• You can hail taxis in the street, or find them at a taxi rank. In some towns you can also order a taxi by phone. In most towns taxis are painted yellow and carry the sign **TAKSİ** on the roof.

• All taxis should have meters and it is a good idea to check that the meter has been turned on at the start of your journey. If you are travelling far, you may negotiate the fare rather than have it metered. In Istanbul the toll for the two bridges over the Bosphorus is not included in the sum you'll see on the meter; the driver will add this to the fare. You may be asked to pay a supplement if you have more than a reasonable amount of luggage. Tipping is not customary unless the driver has provided some other service like carrying your luggage. In that case a tip of 10% or so is usual.

• In some towns shared taxis called **dolmuş** operate on certain routes. You can get on and off the **dolmuş** at any point along its route. The price would be in proportion with the distance you travel.

You may see

Lütfen kapıyı yavaş kapayınız	Please close the door gently
Lütfen sigara içmeyiniz	Please do not smoke
Dolmuş indirme bindirme yeri	Pick-up point for **dolmuş**

You may want to say

(See also Directions, page 25)

I need a taxi
Bir taksi istiyorum
bir taksi istiyorum

Where can I get a taxi?
Nerede taksi bulurum?
nerede taksi bulurum

Could you call me a taxi?
Bana bir taksi çağırır mısınız?
bana bir taksi cha:uhruhr muhsuhnuhz

Immediately
Hemen
hemen

For tomorrow morning at nine o'clock
Yarın sabah saat dokuz için
yaruhn sabah saat dokuz ichin

To the airport, please
Havaalanına lütfen
havaalanuhna lewtfen

To the station, please
İstasyona lütfen
istasyona lewtfen

To the Hotel Etap, please
Etap Oteline lütfen
etap oteline lewtfen

To this address, please
Bu adrese lütfen
bu adrese lewtfen

Is it far?
Uzak mı?
uzakmuh

How much will it cost?
Kaç para tutar?
kach para tutar

I am in a hurry
Acelem var
ajelem var

Stop here, please
Burada durun lütfen
burada durun lewtfen

Could you wait (a few minutes), please?
(Biraz) bekler misiniz?
(biraz) bekler misiniz

How much is it?
Kaç para?
kach para

There is a mistake
Bir yanlışlık var
bir yanluhshluhk var

On the meter it says 20,000
   liras
Saat yirmi bin lira gösteriyor
saat yirmi bin lira gösteriyor

Keep the change
Üstü kalsın
ewstew kalsuhn

That's all right
Tamam
tamam

Could you give me a receipt?
Bir makbuz verir misiniz?
bir makbuz verir misiniz

For 30,000 liras
Otuz bin liralık
otuz bin liraluhk

You may hear

On kilometre kadar uzakta
on kilometre kadar uzakta
It's about 10 kilometres away

Otuz sekiz bin lira
otuz sekiz bin lira
(It's) 38,000 liras

İlave var
ila:ve var
There is a supplement

Köprü için
köprew ichin
(Toll) for the bridge

AIR TRAVEL

● At major airports and all airline offices, you'll find someone who speaks English, but you may still have to say a few things in Turkish.

● There are six international airports (Ankara, Istanbul, Izmir, Antalya, Dalaman, Adana), and Turkish Airlines have regular flights between major cities.

You may see

Aktarma	Transfer
Can yeleği	Life jacket
Çıkış	Exit
Çıkış kapısı	Boarding gate
Çıkış salonu	Departure lounge
Danışma	Information
Dış hatlar	International flights
Gecikme	Delay
Gecikmeli	Delayed
Geliş	Arrival
Gidiş	Departure
Giriş	Entrance
Gümrük	Customs
Gümrük salonu	Customs hall
Güvenlik kontrolu	Security check
Havaalanı	Airport
İç hatlar	Domestic flights
Kambiyo	Bureau de change
Kapı	Gate
Kayıp eşya	Lost property

Kemerlerinizi bağlayınız	Fasten seatbelts
Pasaport kontrolu	Passport control
PTT	Post Office
Sigara içilmez	No smoking
Sigara içmeyiniz	Do not smoke
Tuvalet	Toilet
Uçuş	Flight
Vize	Visa
Yerel saat	Local time
Yolcu salonu	Passenger hall

You may want to say

(See also Numbers, page 189; Days, months, dates, page 170;
Time, page 173)

Is there a flight (from
   Istanbul) to Izmir?
**(İstanbul'dan) İzmir'e uçak
   var mı?**
*(istanbuldan) izmire uchak
   varmuh*

Today
Bugün
bugewn

This morning/afternoon
Bu sabah/öğleden sonra
bu sabah/ö:leden sonra

Tomorrow (morning/
   afternoon)
Yarın (sabah/öğleden sonra)
yaruhn (sabah/ö:leden sonra)

Do you have a timetable of
   flights to Ankara?
**Ankara uçaklarının tarifesi
   var mı?**
*ankara uchaklaruhnuhn
   ta:rifesi varmuh*

What time is the first flight
   to Antalya?
**Antalya'ya ilk uçak saat
   kaçta?**
*antalya-ya ilk uchak saat
   kachta*

The next flight
Bir sonraki uçak
bir sonraki uchak

The last flight
Son uçak
son uchak

What time does it arrive (at Antalya)?
Saat kaçta (Antalya'ya) varıyor?
saat kachta (antalya-ya) varuhyor

A ticket/Two tickets to Dalaman, please
Dalaman'a bir bilet/iki bilet lütfen
dalamana bir bilet/iki bilet lewtfen

Single
Gidiş
gidish

Return
Gidiş dönüş
gidish dönewsh

First class/Business class
Birinci sınıf
birinji suhnuhf

Economy class/Tourist class
Ekonomi/Turist
ekonomi/turist

For the ten o'clock flight
On uçağı için
on ucha:uh ichin

I want to change my reservation
Rezervasyonumu değiştirmek istiyorum
rezervasyonumu de:ishtirmek istiyorum

I want to cancel my reservation
Rezervasyonumu iptal etmek istiyorum
rezervasyonumu iptal etmek istiyorum

What is the number of the flight?
Sefer sayısı kaç?
sefer siyuhsuh kach

What time do I have to check in?
Saat kaçta check-in yaptırmam lazım?
saat kachta chekin yaptuhrmam la:zuhm

Which gate is it?
Hangi kapı?
hangi kapuh

Is there a delay?
Gecikme var mı?
gejikme varmuh

Where is the luggage from the flight from London?
Londra'dan gelen uçaktan çıkan bavullar nerede?
londradan gelen uchaktan chuhkan bavullar nerede

My luggage is not here
Benim bavulum burada yok
benim bavulum burada yok

Is there a bus to the centre of town?
Şehir merkezine otobüs var mı?
shehir merkezine otobews varmuh

You may hear

Cam kenarında mı oturmak istersiniz?
jam kenaruhndamuh oturmak istersiniz
Would you like to sit by the window?

Koridor tarafında mı oturmak istersiniz
koridor tarafuhndamuh oturmak istersiniz
Would you like to sit by the aisle?

Sigara içilen taraf mı, sigara içilmeyen taraf mı?
sigara ichilen tarafmuh, sigara ichilmeyen tarafmuh
Smoking or non-smoking?

Beş numaralı kapı
besh numaraluh kapuh
Gate number five

Pasaportunuz lütfen
pasaportunuz lewtfen
Your passport, please

Biletiniz lütfen
biletiniz lewtfen
Your ticket, please

Biniş kartınız lütfen
binish kartuhnuhz lewtfen
Your boarding card, please

Announcements you may hear over the airport public address system

Words to listen for include:

Dikkat! Dikkat!
dikkat dikkat
Attention! Attention!

Yolcu(lar)
yolju(lar)
Passenger(s)

... sefer sayılı uçak
... sefer siyuhluh uchak
Flight number ...

Kapı
kapuh
Gate

... giden
... giden
Bound for ...

Gecikmeli
gejikmeli
Delayed

Kalkışa hazır
kalkuhsha hazuhr
Ready for take off

İniş
inish
Landing

Son çağrı
son cha:ruh
Last call

TRAVELLING BY TRAIN

● The Turkish State railway company is the **TCDD – Türkiye Cumhuriyeti Devlet Demiryolları**. The railway network is not very extensive and trains are rather slow, but it can be an interesting way of seeing the countryside. On some routes **Mavi Tren** (Blue Trains) operate; these trains are faster.

● Advance booking is advisable for long-distance services, especially for sleeping cars. There are reductions for children and also students.

● Work out in advance what you're going to ask for (1st or 2nd class, single or return, adult or child tickets). If you just ask for 'a ticket' (**bilet**), it'll be assumed that you want a single (**gidiş**) unless you specify 'return' (**gidiş dönüş**).

You may see

Açık	Open
Alt geçit	Subway
Banliyö (hatları)	Suburban (lines)
Bay	Men
Bayan	Women
Bekleme salonu	Waiting room
Bilet	Tickets
Bilet gişesi	Ticket office
Bozuk	Out of order
Dolu	Full, engaged
Emanet	Left luggage
Gar	Station
Hafta sonları	Weekends
Hareket	Departure

İstasyon	Station
Kalkış	Departure
Kapalı	Closed
Kuşet	Couchettes
Meşgul	Engaged
OO	Toilets
Pencereden sarkmayınız	Do not lean out of the window
Ray	Rails
Tatil günleri	Holidays
Tarife	Timetable
TCDD	Turkish Railways
Varış	Arrival
Yataklı	Sleeper
Yataklı vagon	Sleeping car
Yemekli vagon	Dining car
Yer numarası	Seat number
Yolcu treni	Passenger train
Yük treni	Goods train

You may want to say

Information

(See Time, page 173)

Is there a train to Konya?
Konya'ya tren var mı?
konya-ya tren varmuh

Do you have a timetable of trains to Gebze?
Gebze'ye giden trenlerin tarifesi var mı?
gebzeye giden trenlerin ta:rifesi varmuh

What time ...?
... saat kaçta?
... saat kachta

What time is the train to Sivas?
Sivas treni saat kaçta?
sivas treni saat kachta

What time is the first train to Ankara?
Ankara'ya ilk tren saat kaçta?
ankara-ya ilk tren saat kachta

The next train
Bir sonraki tren
bir sonraki tren

The last train
Son tren
son tren

What time does it arrive (at Kars)?
(Kars'a) saat kaçta varıyor?
(karsa) saat kachta varuhyor

What time does the train from Balıkesir arrive?
Balıkesir'den gelen tren saat kaçta burada oluyor?
baluhkesirden gelen tren saat kachta burada oluyor

The train to Diyarbakır, please?
Diyarbakır treni lütfen?
diyarbakuhr treni lewtfen

Which platform does the train to Edirne leave from?
Edirne treni hangi perondan kalkıyor?
edirne treni hangi perondan kalkuhyor

Does this train go to İzmit?
Bu tren İzmit'e gidiyor mu?
bu tren izmite gidiyormu

Do I have to make a change?
Aktarma yapmam lazım mı?
aktarma yapmam la:zuhm-muh

Where?
Nerede?
nerede

Tickets

(See Time, page 173; Numbers, 189 and inside front cover)

One ticket/Two tickets to Tuzla, please
Tuzla'ya bir bilet/iki bilet lütfen
tuzla:ya bir bilet/iki bilet lewtfen

Single
Gidiş
gidish

Return
Gidiş dönüş
gidish dönewsh

For one adult/two adults
Bir tam bilet/İki tam bilet
bir tam bilet/iki tam bilet

(And) one child/two children
(Ve) bir çocuk/iki çocuk
(ve) bir chojuk/iki chojuk

First/Second class
Birinci/İkinci sınıf
birinji/ikinji suhnuhf

For the nine o'clock train
to Adapazarı
**Saat dokuzdaki Adapazarı
treni için**
*saat dokuzdaki adapazaruh
treni ichin*

For the 'Blue Train' to
Ankara
**Ankara'ya giden Mavi Tren
için**
*ankara-ya giden ma:vi tren
ichin*

I want to reserve a seat/
two seats
**Bir kişilik/İki kişilik yer
ayırtmak istiyorum**
*bir kishilik/iki kishilik yer
iyuhrtmak istiyorum*

I want to reserve a sleeper
Bir yatakh ayırtmak istiyorum
*bir yatakluh iyuhrtmak
istiyorum*

I want to reserve a couchette
Bir kuşetli ayırtmak istiyorum
*bir kushetli iyuhrtmak
istiyorum*

Can I take my bicycle on
the train?
**Bisikletimi trene alabilir
miyim?**
*bisikletimi trene alabilir
mi-yim*

How much is it?
Kaç para?
kach para

Left luggage

Can I leave this here?
Bunu burada bırakabilir miyim?
bunu burada buhrakabilir mi-yim

Can I leave these two suitcases here until three o'clock?
Bu iki bavulu saat üçe kadar burada bırakabilir miyim?
bu iki bavulu saat ewche kadar burada buhrakabilir mi-yim

What time do you close?
Saat kaçta kapatıyorsunuz?
saat kachta kapatuhyorsunuz

On the train

I have reserved a seat
Yer ayırttım
yer iyuhrttuhm

I have reserved a sleeper/ couchette
Yataklı/Kuşet ayırttım
yatakluh/kushet iyuhrttuhm

Is this seat free?
Bu yer boş mu?
bu yer boshmu

Do you mind if I open the window?
Pencereyi açabilir miyim?
penjereyi achabilir mi-yim

May I smoke?
Sigara içebilir miyim?
sigara ichebilir mi-yim

Where is the restaurant car?
Yemekli vagon nerede?
yemekli vagon nerede

Where is the sleeping car?
Yataklı vagon nerede?
yatakluh vagon nerede

Excuse me, may I get by?
Affedersiniz, geçebilir miyim?
affedersiniz gechebilir mi-yim

Where are we?
Neredeyiz?
neredeyiz

Are we at Bostancı?
Bostancı'da mıyız?
bostanjuhda muhyuhz

How long does the train stop here?
Tren burada kaç dakika duracak?
tren burada kach dakika durajak

Could you tell me when we get to Haydarpaşa?
Haydarpaşa'ya gelince bana haber verir misiniz?
hiydarpasha:ya gelinje bana haber verir misiniz

You may hear

Information

(See Time, page 173)

On buçukta kalkıyor
on buchukta kalkuhyor
It leaves at half past ten

Beşe çeyrek kala varıyor
beshe cheyrek kala varuhyor
It arrives at a quarter to five

İzmit'te aktarma yapmanız lazım
izmitte aktarma yapmanuhz la:zuhm
You have to change trains at Izmit

Üçüncü peron
ewchewnjew peron
It's platform three

Tickets

Hangi gün için bilet istiyorsunuz?
hangi gewn ichin bilet istiyorsunuz
Which day do you want the ticket for?

Ne zaman gitmek istiyorsunuz?
ne zaman gitmek istiyorsunuz
When do you want to travel?

Gidiş mi, gidiş dönüş mü?
gidishmi gidish dönewshmew
Single or return?

Ne zaman dönüyorsunuz?
ne zaman dönewyorsunuz
When are you coming back?

Seksen beş bin lira
seksen besh bin lira
(It's) 85,000 liras

BUSES AND COACHES

● Buses, minibuses and coaches are the main forms of public transport in Turkey. There is a very limited tram service in Istanbul, although this is gradually being expanded. Istanbul also has a funicular railway between two stops. An underground system is under construction in Ankara, expected to be finished by 1994.

● In major cities you should buy bus tickets at bus station ticket offices, as you cannot pay on the bus. You put your ticket in the box next to the driver by the front door as you get on. At very busy bus stops you may also find people selling bus tickets. In minibuses, which are all run privately, you pay the driver or his assistant during the journey.

● There are very frequent coach services between cities and towns, and minibus services to the villages. Tickets for these long-distance services are bought at ticket offices at the bus stations. Sometimes fares are collected on board.

You may see

Bilet	Ticket
Biniş	Boarding
Çıkış	Exit
Durak	Bus stop
Giriş	Entrance
Gişe	Ticket office
Metro	Underground railway
Oturacak yer	Seat
Otobüs	Bus
Otogar	Coach station

Paso	Pass (for free or reduced travel)
Sigara içilmez	No smoking
Şoförle konuşmak yasaktır	It is forbidden to speak to the driver
Tarife	Timetable
Tramvay	Tram
Tünel	Funicular
Yolcu sayısı	Number of passengers

You may want to say

Information

(For sightseeing bus tours, see Sightseeing, page 121)

Where is the bus stop?
Durak nerede?
durak nerede

Where is the bus/coach station?
Otogar nerede?
otogar nerede

Is there a bus to the beach?
Plaja otobüs var mı?
plazha otobews varmuh

Which bus goes to the station?
İstasyona hangi otobüs gidiyor?
istasyona hangi otobews gidiyor

Will it come soon?
Çabuk gelir mi?
chabuk gelirmi

What time is the bus to Bursa?
Bursa otobüsü saat kaçta?
bursa otobewsew saat kachta

What time is the first bus to Fethiye?
Fethiye'ye ilk otobüs saat kaçta?
fet-hiyeye ilk otobews saat kachta

The next bus
Bir sonraki otobüs
bir sonraki otobews

The last bus
Son otobüs
son otobews

What time does it arrive?
Saat kaçta varıyor?
saat kachta varuhyor

Where does the bus to the town centre leave from?
Şehir merkezine otobüs nereden kalkıyor?
shehir merkezine otobews nereden kalkuhyor

Does the bus to the airport leave from here?
Havaalanına giden otobüs buradan mı kalkıyor?
havaalanuhna giden otobews buradan muh kalkuhyor

Does this bus go to Taksim?
Bu otobüs Taksim'e gidiyor mu?
bu otobews taksime gidiyormu

I want to get off at the museum
Müzede inmek istiyorum
mewzede inmek istiyorum

Could you tell me where to get off?
İneceğim yerde haber verir misiniz?
ineje:im yerde haber verir-misiniz

Should I get off here for the mosque?
Cami için burada mı inmem lazım?
ja:mi ichin burada muh inmem la:zuhm

The next stop, please
Bir sonraki durak lütfen
bir sonraki durak lewtfen

Could you open the door, please?
Kapıyı açar mısınız lütfen?
kapuhyuh achar muhsuhnuhz lewtfen

Excuse me, could I get past?
Affedersiniz, geçebilir miyim?
affedersiniz gechebilir mi-yim

Tickets

Where can I buy bus tickets?
Otobüs bileti nereden alabilirim?
otobews bileti nereden alabilirim

Ten, please
On tane, lütfen
on ta:ne lewtfen

One/two to the town centre, please
Şehir merkezine bir kişi/iki kişi lütfen
shehir merkezine bir kishi/iki kishi lewtfen

How much is it?
Kaç para?
kach para

You may hear

Şehir merkezine (giden) otobüs şuradaki duraktan kalkıyor
shehir merkezine (giden) otobews shuradaki duraktan kalkuhyor
The bus (going) to the town centre leaves from that stop there

On dört numara istasyona gidiyor
on dört numara istasyona gidiyor
Number 14 goes to the station

On dakikada bir var
on dakikada bir var
There is one every ten minutes

On biri yirmi geçe kalkıyor
onbiri yirmi geche kalkuhyor
It leaves at twenty past eleven

Altıya beş kala varıyor
altuhya besh kala varuhyor
It arrives at five to six

Şoföre vereceksiniz
shoföre verejeksiniz
You pay the driver

Burada mı ineceksiniz?
buradamuh inejeksiniz
Are you getting off here?

Bundan sonraki durakta` ineceksiniz
bundan sonraki durakta inejeksiniz
You get off at the next stop

Bir önceki durakta inmeniz lazımdı
bir önjeki durakta inmeniz la:zuhmduh
You should have got off at the previous stop

SHIPS AND FERRIES

● There are two bridges over the Bosphorus in Istanbul, but you can also cross by ship, and there are car ferry services across the Dardanelles (the straits at the western end of the Sea of Marmara, where it joins the Aegean). There are ships that ferry commuters up and down the Bosphorus, stopping at the villages on each side, and ships connecting the centre of Istanbul with the Princes' Islands in the Sea of Marmara. Some of the more distant suburbs can be reached by jetfoil. For almost all commuter travel by sea in Istanbul, you have to buy metal tokens called **jeton**. These are available at the **gişe** (ticket offices) at the landing points.

● The Turkish Maritime Lines runs ships from Istanbul along the Black Sea Coast, and from Istanbul to Izmir and to the Mediterranean ports. There is a twice weekly car ferry service between Istanbul and Izmir, and a weekly one between Istanbul and Venice.

You may see

Araba vapuru	Car ferry
Cankurtaran sandalı	Lifeboat
Cankurtaran simidi	Life belt
Can yeleği	Life jacket
Feribot	Car ferry
Gemi	Ship, boat
İskele	Landing place, berth
Kış tarifesi	Winter timetable
Rıhtım	Quay
Tarife	Timetable

Vapur	Ship, boat
Vapur gezileri	Boat trips
Yaz tarifesi	Summer timetable

You may want to say

Information

(See Time, page 173)

Is there a boat to
  Bandırma (today)?
**Bandırma'ya (bugün) vapur
  var mı?**
*banduhrmaya (bugewn)
  vapur varmuh*

Is there a car ferry to Izmir?
İzmir'e feribot var mı?
izmire feribot varmuh

Are there any boat trips?
Vapur gezileri var mı?
vapur gezileri varmuh

What time is the boat to
  Kadıköy?
Kadıköy vapuru saat kaçta?
kaduhköy vapuru saat kachta

What time is the first boat?
İlk vapur saat kaçta?
ilk vapur saat kachta

The next boat
Bir sonraki vapur
bir sonraki vapur

The last boat
Son vapur
son vapur

What time does it arrive?
Saat kaçta varıyor?
saat kachta varuhyor

What time does it return?
Saat kaçta dönüyor?
saat kachta dönewyor

How long does it take?
Ne kadar sürüyor?
ne kadar sewrewyor

Where does the boat to
  Yalova leave from?
**Yalova vapuru nereden
  kalkıyor?**
*yalova vapuru nereden
  kalkuhyor*

Where can I buy tickets?
Nereden bilet alabilirim?
nereden bilet alabilirim

What is the sea like today?
Deniz bugün nasıl?
deniz bugewn nasuhl

Tickets

(See Numbers, inside front cover)

Four tickets to Bostancı
please
Bostancı'ya dört bilet lütfen
bostanjuhya dört bilet lewtfen

Two adults and two
children
İki tam bilet, iki çocuk
iki tam bilet iki chojuk

Single
Gidiş
gidish·

Return
Gidiş dönüş
gidish dönewsh

I'd like to buy tickets for
the car ferry to Izmir
**İzmir'e giden feribot için
bilet almak istiyorum**
*izmire giden feribot ichin
bilet almak istiyorum*

A car and two passengers
Bir araba ve iki yolcu
bir araba ve iki yolju

How much is it?
Kaç para?
kach para

You may hear

Çarşamba ve Cuma günleri vapur var
charshamba ve juma gewnleri vapur var
There are boats on Wednesdays and Fridays

Avşa'ya giden vapur saat dokuzda kalkıyor
avsha-ya giden vapur saat dokuzda kalkuhyor
The boat that goes to Avşa leaves at nine o'clock

Saat dört buçukta dönüyor
saat dört buchukta dönewyor
It returns at half past four

İzmir'e giden vapur Sirkeci'den kalkıyor
izmire giden vapur sirkejiden kalkuhyor
The boat to Izmir leaves from Sirkeci

Deniz sakin
deniz sa:kin
The sea is calm

Deniz dalgalı
deniz dalgaluh
The sea is rough

AT THE TOURIST OFFICE

• There are tourist information offices in most towns and cities popular with tourists – look for the sign **Turizm Danışma**. Usually there is someone who speaks English in these offices, where you will find leaflets about local sights, lists of hotels, maps of the town and the region. Information can be provided about opening times and local transport.

• Tourist offices in major cities are usually open between 9 a.m. and 7 p.m., although some close at lunch time (12.00–1.30 p.m.).

You may want to say

(See Directions, page 25; Sightseeing, page 121; Time, page 173)

Where is the tourist office?
Turizm Danışma Bürosu nerede?
turizm danuhshma bewrosu nerede

Do you speak English?
İngilizce biliyor musunuz?
ingilizje biliyor musunuz

Do you have ...?
... var mı?
... varmuh

Do you have a plan of the city?
Şehir planı var mı?
shehir planuh varmuh

Do you have a map of the area?
Bu yörenin haritası var mı?
bu yörenin haritasuh varmuh

Do you have a list of hotels?
Bir otel listesi var mı?
bir otel listesi varmuh

Do you have a list of campsites?
Bir kamping listesi var mı?
bir kamping listesi varmuh

Could you recommend a cheap hotel?
Ucuz bir otel tavsiye eder misiniz?
ujuz bir otel tavsiye eder misiniz

Could you book a room for me please?
Benim için bir oda ayırtır mısınız?
benim ichin bir oda iyuhrtuhr muhsuhnuhz

Could you recommend a restaurant?
Bir lokanta tavsiye eder misiniz?
bir lokanta tavsiye eder misiniz

Where can I hire a car?
Nereden bir araba kiralayabilirim?
nereden bir araba kira:layabilirim

What is there to see here?
Burada görülecek neresi var?
burada görewlejek neresi var

Do you have any leaflets?
Broşürleriniz var mı?
broshewrleriniz varmuh

Do you have any information about ...?
... hakkında bilginiz var mı?
... hakkuhnda bilginiz varmuh

Where's the archaeological museum?
Arkeoloji müzesi nerede?
arkeolozhi mewzesi nerede

Could you show me on the map?
Haritada bana gösterir misiniz?
haritada bana gösterir misiniz

When's the museum open?
Müze ne zaman açık?
mewze ne zaman achuhk

Are there any excursions?
Geziler var mı?
geziler varmuh

You may hear

(Size) yardım edebilir miyim?
(size) yarduhm edebilir mi-yim
Can I help (you)?

Yardıma ihtiyacınız var mı?
yarduhma ihtiya:juhnuhz varmuh
Do you need help?

İngiliz misiniz?
ingiliz misiniz
Are you English?

Nerelisiniz?
nerelisiniz
Where are you from?

Buyurun
buyurun
Here you are

Burada ne kadar kalacaksınız?
burada ne kadar kalajaksuhnuhz
How long are you staying here?

Hangi otelde kalıyorsunuz?
hangi otelde kaluhyorsunuz
Which hotel are you staying in?

Nasıl bir otel istiyorsunuz?
nasuhl bir otel istiyorsunuz
What kind of hotel would you like?

Deniz kenarında
deniz kenaruhnda
By the sea

(Haritada) burada
(haritada) burada
It's here (on the map)

ACCOMMODATION

● Turkey has a wide range of hotel accommodation. For details, contact the Turkish Tourist Office in London (address, page 187), or in Turkey the Tourist Information Offices in major cities.

● Hotels are usually graded into classes, such as **lüks** (luxury), **birinci sınıf** (first class), **ikinci sınıf** (second class) and so on. There's also a system of stars, but this tends to be restricted to luxury hotels of the 4- or 5-star category.

● In coastal resort areas, you will find a large number of **pansiyon** (guest houses). These are cheaper and generally more personal.

● Local tourist offices can give you lists of hotels in the vicinity or make suggestions about accommodation.

● If you go camping, it is best and safest to stay at official campsites. The tourist offices will provide lists and details about these sites. If you want to camp elsewhere, make sure that it is an area where camping is allowed. It may be a forest fire danger area or within a military zone.

● If you are travelling in parts of the country which are not major tourist areas, it's best to avoid the cheapest hotels in smaller towns, even if you are keen to save money, as they are not geared to foreign tourists. In most places, you will find reasonably-priced, secure and comfortable accommodation with a private shower in the medium price category.

You may see

Asansör	Lift
Askeri bölge	Military zone
Asma kat	Mezzanine floor
Ateş yakmak yasaktır	It is forbidden to light fires (No naked flames)
Banyo	Bath
Birinci kat	First floor
Bodrum	Basement
Çamaşır	Laundry
Çatı	Roof
Çıkış	Exit
Çöp	Rubbish
Dolu	Full
Duş	Shower
Fiyat listesi	Price list
Giriş	Entry
İçme suyu	Drinking water
İkinci kat	Second floor
Kahvaltı	Breakfast
Oda servisi	Room service
Orman yangını tehlike bölgesi	Forest fire danger area
Otel	Hotel
Pansiyon	Guest House
Resepsiyon	Reception
Restoran/Lokanta	Restaurant
Tam pansiyon	Full board
Tarife	Price list
Tehlike	Danger
Televizyon salonu	Television room
Yangın merdiveni	Fire escape
Yangın tehlikesi	Fire hazard
Yarım pansiyon	Half board

Yatak	Bed
Yemek salonu	Dining room
Yüzme havuzu	Swimming pool
Zemin kat	Ground floor

You may want to say

Booking in and out

I've reserved a room
Bir oda ayırtmıştım
bir oda iyuhrtmuhshtuhm

I've reserved two rooms
İki oda ayırtmıştım
iki oda iyuhrtmuhshtuhm

I've reserved a place
Yer ayırtmıştım
yer iyuhrtmuhshtuhm

My name is ...
İsmim ...
ismim ...

Do you have a room vacant?
Boş odanız var mı?
bosh odanuhz varmuh

Do you have a single/
double room?
**Tek kişilik/İki kişilik odanız
var mı?**
*tek kishilik/iki kishilik
odanuhz varmuh*

A single room
Tek kişilik bir oda
tek kishilik bir oda

A double room
İki kişilik bir oda
iki kishilik bir oda

For one night
Bir gece için
bir geje ichin

For two nights
İki gece için
iki geje ichin

With bath/shower
Banyolu/Duşlu
banyolu/dushlu

Can I see the room?
Odayı görebilir miyim?
odiyuh görebilir mi-yim

Do you have space for a tent?
Bir çadır için yeriniz var mı?
bir chaduhr ichin yeriniz varmuh

Do you have space for a caravan?
Bir treyler için yeriniz var mı?
bir treyler ichin yeriniz varmuh

How much is it?
Kaç para?
kach para

Per night
Bir gecesi
bir gejesi

Per week
Bir haftası
bir haftasuh

Is there a reduction for children?
Çocuklar için indirim var mı?
chojuklar ichin indirim varmuh

Is breakfast included?
Kahvaltı dahil mi?
kahvaltuh da:hilmi

It's too expensive
Çok pahalı
chok pahaluh

Do you have anything cheaper?
Daha ucuzu var mı?
daha ujuzu varmuh

Do you have anything bigger/anything smaller?
Daha büyüğü/Daha küçüğü var mı?
daha bewyew:ew/daha kewchew:ew varmuh

I'd like to stay another night
Bir gece daha kalmak istiyorum
bir geje daha kalmak istiyorum

I am leaving tomorrow morning
Yarın sabah ayrılıyorum
yaruhn sabah iyruhluhyorum

The bill, please
Hesap lütfen
hesap lewtfen

Do you take credit cards?
Kredi kartı alıyor musunuz?
kredi kartuh aluhyor musunuz

Do you take travellers' cheques?
Seyahat çeki alıyor musunuz?
seyahat cheki aluhyor musunuz

Could you recommend a hotel in Kemer?
Kemer'de bir otel tavsiye eder misiniz?
kemerde bir otel tavsi-ye eder misiniz

Could you phone them to make a booking?
Yer ayırtmak için telefon eder misiniz?
yer iyuhrtmak ichin telefon eder misiniz

In hotels

(See Problems and complaints, page 147; Time, page 173)

Where can I park?
Arabayı nerede park edebilirim?
arabiyuh nerede park edebilirim

Do you have a cot for the baby?
Bebek yatağınız var mı?
bebek yata:uhnuhz varmuh

Is there room service?
Oda servisi var mı?
oda servisi varmuh

Do you have facilities for the disabled?
Sakatlar için özel imkanlar var mı?
sakatlar ichin özel imkanlar varmuh

What time is breakfast?
Kahvaltı saat kaçta?
kahvaltuh saat kachta

Can I have breakfast in the room?
Odada kahvaltı edebilir miyim?
odada kahvaltuh edebilir mi-yim

What time is dinner?
Akşam yemeği saat kaçta?
aksham yeme:i saat kachta

What time does the hotel close?
Otel gece saat kaçta kapanıyor?
otel geje saat kachta kapanuhyor

I'll be back very late
Çok geç geleceğim
chok gech geleje:im

(Key) number 42, please
Kırk iki numara (anahtarı) lütfen
kuhrk iki numara (anahtaruh) lewtfen

Are there any messages for me?
Bana mesaj var mı?
bana mesazh varmuh

Where's the bathroom/toilet?
Banyo/Tuvalet nerede?
banyo/tuvalet nerede

Where's the dining room?
Yemek salonu nerede?
yemek salonu nerede

Can I leave this in the safe?
Bunu kasaya koyabilir miyim?
bunu kasaya koyabilir mi-yim

Could you get my things from the safe?
Kasadaki eşyalarımı çıkarır mısınız?
kasadaki eshya:laruhmuh chuhkaruhr muhsuhnuhz

Could you wake me up at eight o'clock?
Beni saat sekizde uyandırır mısınız?
beni saat sekizde uyanduhruhr muhsuhnuhz

Could you call me a taxi?
Bana bir taksi çağırır mısınız?
bana bir taksi cha:uhruhr muhsuhnuhz

For right now
Hemen şimdi
hemen shimdi

For tomorrow morning at nine o'clock
Yarın sabah saat dokuz için
yaruhn sabah saat dokuz ichin

Could you have my suit cleaned?
Elbisemi temizletir misiniz?
elbisemi temizletir misiniz

Could you find me a baby-sitter?
Çocuğa bakacak birisini bulur musunuz?
choju:a bakajak birisini bulur musunuz

Could you put it on the bill, please?
Hesaba yazın lütfen
hesaba yazuhn lewtfen

I need another pillow
Bir yastık daha istiyorum
bir yastuhk daha istiyorum

I need a towel
Bir havlu istiyorum
bir havlu istiyorum

73

At campsites

Is there a campsite around here?
Buralarda bir kamp yeri var mı?
buralarda bir kamp yeri varmuh

Can I camp here?
Burada kamp yapabilir miyim?
burada kamp yapabilir mi-yim

Where can I park?
Nerede park edebilirim?
nerede park edebilirim

Where are the showers?
Duş nerede?
dush nerede

Where are the toilets?
Tuvalet nerede?
tuvalet nerede

Where are the dustbins?
Çöp tenekeleri nerede?
chöp tenekeleri nerede

Is the water drinkable?
Su içilir mi?
su ichilirmi

Where is the laundry room?
Çamaşırlık nerede?
chamashuhrluhk nerede

Where is the electricity point?
Elektrik prizi nerede?
elektrik prizi nerede

Self-catering accommodation

(See Directions, page 25; Problems and complaints, page 147)

I have rented a villa
Bir villa kiraladım
bir villa kira:laduhm

I have rented an apartment
Bir daire kiraladım
bir daire kira:laduhm

We're in number 11
On bir numaradayız
on bir numaradayuhz

My name is ...
İsmim ...
ismim ...

What's the address?
Adres ne?
adres ne

How do I get there?
Oraya nasıl giderim?
oriya nasuhl giderim

Could you give me the key?
Anahtarı verir misiniz?
anahtaruh verir misiniz

Where is ...?
... nerede?
... nerede

Where is the stopcock?
Vana nerede?
vana nerede

Where is the fuse-box?
Sigorta nerede?
sigorta nerede

How does the cooker work?
Ocak nasıl çalışıyor?
ojak nasuhl chaluhshuhyor

How does the water-heater
    work?
Şofben nasıl çalışıyor?
shofben nasuhl chaluhshuhyor

Is there air-conditioning?
Havalandırma var mı?
havalanduhrma varmuh

Is there a spare gas bottle?
Yedek tüp var mı?
yedek tewp varmuh

Is there any more bedding?
Başka yatak takımı var mı?
*bashka yatak takuhmuh
    varmuh*

What day do they come to
    clean?
Temizlikçi hangi gün geliyor?
temizlikchi hangi gewn geliyor

Where do I put the rubbish?
Çöpü nereye koyacağım?
chöpew nereye koyaja:uhm

When do they come to
    collect the rubbish?
**Çöpü almaya ne zaman
    geliyorlar?**
*chöpew almuhya ne zaman
    geliyorlar*

Where can I contact you?
Sizi nerede bulabilirim?
sizi nerede bulabilirim

(Size) yardım edebilir miyim?
*(size) yarduhm edebilir
  mi-yim*
Can I help you?

İsminiz lütfen
isminiz lewtfen
Your name please

Kaç gece için?
kach geje ichin
For how many nights?

Kaç kişilik?
kach kishilik
For how many people?

Banyolu mu, banyosuz mu?
banyolumu banyosuzmu
With or without bath?

Çadır büyük mü, küçük mü?
*chaduhr bewyewkmew
  kewchewkmew*
Is the tent large or small?

Maalesef, doluyuz
maalesef doluyuz
I'm sorry, we're full

Pasaportunuz lütfen
pasaportunuz lewtfen
Your passport, please

(Burayı) imzalayın
(buriyuh) imza:layuhn
Sign (here)

Böyle açıyorsunuz
böyle achuhyorsunuz
You turn it on like this

Böyle kapıyorsunuz
böyle kapuhyorsunuz
You turn it off like this

Her gün geliyorlar
her gewn geliyorlar
They come every day

Cumartesi günleri geliyorlar
jumartesi gewnleri geliyorlar
They come on Saturdays

76

TELEPHONES

- There are telephone boxes in the streets and payphones in most restaurants and cafés. Telephone boxes where you can call abroad are usually marked **milletlerarası** – 'international'. Most public phones have instructions in English as well as Turkish. You can also make long-distance calls from post offices.

- Older public telephones are operated with tokens, **jeton**, that you can buy at post offices and some newsagents and tobacconists. They come in three values and sizes: **küçük** (small), **orta** (medium) and **büyük** (large). You lift the receiver, put the token in the appropriate slot and dial – if you don't get through, you'll get the token back. For phoning abroad, you'll need a large token or a number of medium ones. You can then put in more tokens while you are talking. A small red light will warn you when to put in more.

- Telephones operated by phonecards are becoming widely available, and it is easier to make international calls from these phones. You can buy phonecards at post offices, some newsagents and hotel receptions.

- To call abroad, first dial 99, followed by the code for the country – it's 44 for the UK. Follow this with the town code, minus the initial 0, and then the number you want. For example, to get a central London number, you dial 99 44 71 and then the 7-digit number. The number for the international operator in Turkey is 032. You can use this number to make a reverse charge call to the UK.

- To call inter-city in Turkey, you dial 9, followed by the area code: for Istanbul it's 1, and for Ankara 4. Then you dial the number you require.

Instructions you may see in a phone box:

Ahizeyi kaldırın	Lift the receiver
Jetonu atın	Put in the token
Kırmızı ışık sönünce	When the red light goes off
Numarayı çevirin	Dial the number
Dokuzu çevirin	Dial 9

You may see

Bozuk	Out of order
Jeton	Token
Kod numarası	Code
Milletlerarası	International
Santral	Exchange
Şehirlerarası	Inter-city (in Turkey)
Telefon	Telephone
Telefon kartı	Phonecard
Telefon rehberi	Telephone directory

You may want to say

Is there a telephone?
Telefon var mı?
telefon varmuh

Where is the telephone?
Telefon nerede?
telefon nerede

Four large tokens, please.
Dört büyük jeton lütfen.
dört bewyewk zheton lewtfen

A phonecard please
Bir telefon kartı lütfen
bir telefon kartuh lewtfen

Do you have a telephone directory?
Bir telefon rehberi var mı?
bir telefon rehberi varmuh

I want to call the UK
İngiltere'ye telefon etmek istiyorum
ingiltereye telefon etmek istiyorum

Mr Sevgen, please
Bay Sevgen lütfen
biy sevgen lewtfen

Extension 213, please
İki yüz on üç numara lütfen
iki yewz on ewch numara lewtfen

My name is ...
İsmim ...
ismim ...

I am ...
Ben ...
ben ...

When will he/she be back?
Ne zaman döner?
ne zaman döner

I'll call later
Sonra ararım
sonra araruhm

Can I hold, please?
Bekleyebilir miyim?
bekleyebilir mi-yim

Can I leave a message, please?
Bir mesaj bırakabilir miyim?
bir mesazh buhrakabilir mi-yim

Please tell him/her that I called – my name is ...
Lütfen aradığımı söyleyin – ismim ...
lewtfen araduh:uhmuh söyleyin – ismim ...

I'm staying in the Hotel Marmara
Marmara Otelinde kalıyorum
marmara otelinde kaluhyorum

My telephone number is ...
Telefon numaram ...
telefon numaram...

Could you ask him/her to call me?
Beni aramasını söyler misiniz?
beni aramasuhnuh söyler misiniz

Could you repeat that please?
Tekrarlar mısınız?
tekrarlar muhsuhnuz

More slowly, please
Daha yavaş lütfen
daha yavash lewtfen

Sorry, I've got the wrong number
Affedersiniz, yanlış
affedersiniz yanluhsh

We've been cut off/The line's gone dead
Telefon kesildi
telefon kesildi

How much is the call?
Telefon görüşmesi kaç para?
telefon görewshmesi kach para

What number should I dial to call a taxi?
Taksi çağrmak için hangi numarayı aramam lazım?
taksi cha:uhrmak ichin hangi numariyuh aramam la:zuhm

You may hear

Alo!
alo:
Hello!

Buyurun!/Efendim!
buyurun/efendim
Yes?

Kim arıyor?
kim aruhyor
Who's calling?

Bir dakika lütfen
bir dakika lewtfen
One moment, please

Kapatmayın
kapatmayuhn
Hold the line

Bekleyin lütfen
bekleyin lewtfen
Please wait

Bağlıyorum
ba:luhyorum
I'm putting you through

Meşgul
meshgul
(It's) engaged

Hat meşgul
hat meshgul
The line's engaged

Bekler misiniz?
bekler misiniz
Do you want to hold on?

Cevap yok
jevap yok
No reply

Kendisi yok
kendisi yok
He/she's not here

Yanlış (numara)
yanluhsh (numara)
Wrong number

CHANGING MONEY

● The Turkish unit of currency is the lira – you'll see it abbreviated as TL, short for **Türk Lirası**, 'Turkish Lira'.

● You can change foreign currency or travellers' cheques into lira at most banks and at other places where you see the sign **KAMBİYO**.

● Banks are open from 9 a.m. until 5.30 p.m. Mondays–Fridays, with a lunch break 12.30–1.30 p.m. or longer, but if you need to change money or cash travellers' cheques, it is best to do it before 4 p.m. as most banks stop doing such transactions around that time.

● In banks you go first to the counter marked **kambiyo**. You'll probably have to sign a form and you may be asked for the name of the hotel or the address you're staying at. You may get your lira at the same counter – or you may have to go to the **vezne** (cashier).

You may see

Açık	Open
Banka	Bank
Bankamatik	Cash dispenser
Çalışma saatleri	Hours of business
Çekiniz	Pull
Çıkış	Exit
Döviz	Foreign currency
Giriş	Entrance
İtiniz	Push
Kambiyo	Change, bureau de change
Kapalı	Closed
Öğle tatili	Lunch break
Vezne	Cashier

You may want to say

I'd like to change some pounds sterling
Sterlin bozdurmak istiyorum
sterlin bozdurmak istiyorum

I'd like to change some travellers' cheques
Seyahat çeki bozdurmak istiyorum
seyahat cheki bozdurmak istiyorum

I'd like to get some money with this credit card
Bu kredi kartı ile para çekmek istiyorum
bu kredi kartuh ile para chekmek istiyorum

What's the exchange rate today?
Kur bugün ne kadar?
kur bugewn ne kadar

Could you give me some change, please?
Biraz bozuk para verir misiniz?
biraz bozuk para verir misiniz

I'm at the Hotel Çelik Palas
Çelik Palas Otelinde kalıyorum
chelik palas otelinde kaluhyorum

I'm at the Güneş Apartments
Güneş Sitesinde kalıyorum
gewnesh sitesinde kaluhyorum

I'm staying with friends
Arkadaşlarımda kalıyorum
arkadashlaruhmda kaluhyorum

The address is Gölgeli Sokak, 31/5
Adres Gölgeli Sokak, otuz bir taksim beş
adres gölgeli sokak otuz bir taksim besh

You may hear

Ne kadar bozdurmak istiyorsunuz?
ne kadar bozdurmak istiyorsunuz
How much do you want to change?

Pasaportunuz lütfen
pasaportunuz lewtfen
Your passport, please

Adresiniz?
adresiniz
Your address?

Otelinizin adı ne?
otelinizin aduh ne
What's the name of your hotel?

Hangi otelde kalıyorsunuz?
hangi otelde kaluhyorsunuz
Which hotel are you staying in?

Burayı imzalayın
buriyuh imza:liyuhn
Sign here

Lütfen vezneye gidin
lewtfen vezneye gidin
Please go to the cashier

Paranızı vezneden alacaksınız
paranuhzuh vezneden alajaksuhnuhz
You get your money from the cashier

EATING AND DRINKING

● The simplest way to order something is just to name it. You can add **lütfen** (please). If you're ordering for others as well, you can say **bana** (for me) or **ona** (for him/her) to show who wants what.

● If you're ordering more than one of something, just add the number you want before the word, e.g. **bir çay** (one tea), **iki çay** (two teas), **üç bira** (three beers).

● You can order tea, Turkish coffee and soft drinks almost everywhere in Turkey. Tea is the most popular drink; it's traditionally drunk without milk in small glasses, although in big hotels and popular tourist resorts you can ask for **sütlü çay** (tea with milk). You can ask for your tea to be weak (**açık**) or strong (**koyu**), and with lemon (**limonlu**). Herbal teas are also available in some places: **ıhlamur** (linden-blossom tea), **elmaçayı** (apple tea).

● When you order **kahve** (coffee) you'll usually be given Turkish coffee unless you ask for **neskahve** (instant coffee); if you want a white coffee, ask for **bir sütlü neskahve**. You won't find any other kind of coffee except in some luxury cafés and hotels. Turkish coffee is served in small cups without milk, with the sugar added before it's brewed. So you need to say how sweet you want it: **şekerli** (sweet), **az şekerli** (with a little sugar), **orta** (medium sweet), **çok şekerli** (very sweet) or **sade** (no sugar).

● Some cafés serve alcoholic drinks – the most popular is **bira** (beer). The beer is generally what we call lager, and it's sold in bottles or cans. You may be asked which of several brands you want. Some firms also produce **fıçı bira** (draught beer) – also lager-type. In luxury cafés and hotels and in some tourist resorts you'll find other alcoholic drinks – the most common are **cin** (gin) and **votka** (vodka). **Tonik** (tonic water) and **vermut** (vermouth) are also popular. The other principal drinks are **kanyak** (brandy) and **viski** (whisky). These can either be **yerli** (locally produced) or **ithal** (imported). People in Turkey don't usually drink wine or **rakı** (aniseed-flavoured spirit like the Greek **ouzo**), unless they're eating a meal.

● Traditional tea-houses (**çayhane**) serve only tea, coffee and a few soft drinks and are not usually patronised by women, although tourists of both sexes are welcome.

● You normally pay in cafés and restaurants when you're ready to leave, though in some self-service cafés, ice-cream parlours and snack-bars you may have to pay at the till in advance.

● Restaurants (**restoran** or **lokanta**) are classified into different categories, reflecting the range and prices of the dishes offered. The categories are luxury (**lüks**), first class (**birinci sınıf**), second class (**ikinci sınıf**) and third class (**üçüncü sınıf**) – the class is normally indicated at the entrance and on the menu. Restaurant prices include VAT (**KDV**) and often service (**servis**), but an extra tip of about 5% is appreciated. Where service isn't included, 12% is about right for the tip.

● Breakfast is served between 6.30 or 7.00 and 10.00 a.m., lunch between 12.00 and 2.00 p.m. and dinner between 7.00 and 10.00 p.m., though cheaper restaurants often start serving earlier in the evening and close earlier. In rural areas, it may be difficult to get a proper meal after 8.00 p.m. or even earlier in the winter.

● During the fasting month of **Ramazan** (Ramadan, which falls between different dates each year), pious Moslems don't eat or drink during daylight hours, and in traditional areas you may find it difficult to get a meal during the day, although you'll have no problems in the big cities or in tourist resorts. In traditional areas during **Ramazan**, the restaurants open after sunset, and as soon as they start serving there's a tremendous rush – if you don't eat then you're likely to find there's little left later on, although you'll find tea-houses and cafés stay open much later than at other times of the year.

● Breakfast in Turkey usually consists of tea, with bread or toast, butter, jam or honey, cheese and black olives, and you can ask for **yumurta** (eggs), either **rafadan** (soft-boiled) or **yağda** (fried). You'll often see cheap restaurants open at breakfast time, serving soup.

● There's great variety in Turkish food and you'll find the widest choice in the big cities. A typical meal would start with soup, followed by a meat dish with rice or potatoes, often with a side salad. There would then be a vegetable dish and a sweet dish or fruit at the end of the meal. Vegetable dishes are plentiful, but strict vegetarians should ask for them to be **zeytinyağlı** (cooked with olive oil) rather than cooked in meat stock (**et suyu**). Turkish food is not generally spicy (except for some kebabs). You won't find any pork dishes on the menu anywhere, except in a few specialist restaurants in Istanbul.

● In the evenings, you'll find restaurants serving **meze**, a selection of hors d'œuvres. These are normally eaten as an accompaniment to drinking; the most popular drink for this is **rakı**, a strong aniseed-flavoured spirit that you can drink with ice and/or water. When it's diluted, it turns cloudy, like the Greek **ouzo**. This kind of restaurant often serves grilled meat or fish as a main course after the **meze**.

● There are lots of kebab houses (**kebapçı**) in Turkey. The most elaborate are called **et lokantası** and offer a wide selection of different grilled meats. The most common kebabs are **şiş kebap** (small pieces of lamb grilled on small skewers) and **şiş köfte** (minced lamb in small strips, grilled on a metal skewer). **Döner kebap** – the name means 'turning kebab' – is pieces of lamb pressed on to a large, vertical metal skewer which stands in front of a fire; as the outer layer cooks, it's shaved off and served, often **yoğurtlu** (with yoghurt), although you can ask for it **yoğurtsuz** (without yoghurt) or **sade** (by itself). If you ask for **iskender kebap**, you'll get slices of **döner kebap** served with tomato purée and yoghurt, on a bed of **pide** (pitta bread). Other common kinds of kebab include **çöp kebap** – tiny pieces of grilled lamb cooked very quickly. **Pide** is frequently served with all kinds of kebab.

● In coastal towns and seaside resorts, fresh fish is usually available – it's best to go to a **balık lokantası** (fish restaurant) if you want to be sure of getting good, fresh fish. You'll also find good fish restaurants in Ankara. Fish can be expensive, and it may be best to ask the price before you order it, if it is not shown on the menu. The price often depends on the weight of the portion you order. You'll often be asked how you want the fish cooked – usually **ızgara** (grilled) or **tava** (fried).

● Turkish cuisine has a rich choice of sweet dishes, pastries, cakes and puddings. The most famous is **baklava** – layers of very thin pastry, interspersed with crushed walnuts or pistachio nuts and steeped in syrup.

● Wine is produced in Thrace (the European part of Turkey), the Aegean region and Central Anatolia – there's a large number of brand names. Turkish wine is best drunk young. White (**beyaz**), red (**kırmızı**) and rosé (**roze**) wines are generally all good when young, and you'll also find **köpüklü şarap** (sparkling wine), which is sometimes called **şampanya**. Most wine is **sek** (dry), but you'll find some marked **dömi-sek** (medium dry). Dry sparkling wine is usually marked **brüt**.

● In the cheapest restaurants, you'll usually only find **su** (water). Elsewhere, though, you'll find a category on the menu called **meşrubat** (non-alcoholic drinks), which will include **maden suyu** (mineral water), **meyve suyu** (fruit juice), and **gazoz** (fizzy lemonade). Another popular drink is **ayran** – yoghurt mixed with salt and water and served ice-cold. Tea and Turkish coffee are usually available after a meal, but often they're brought to your table from the local tea-house.

You may see

Aile lokantası	Family restaurant
Balık lokantası	Fish restaurant
Çay bahçesi	Tea garden
Çayhane	Tea house
Et lokantası	Meat restaurant
Günün yemeği	Dish of the day
Hergün açık	Open every day
İçkisiz	No alcohol served
Kebapçı	Kebab house
Kıraathane	Traditional café
Lokanta	Restaurant
Meşrubat	Non-alcoholic drinks
Pastane	Patisserie, luxury café
Pazar günleri kapalı	Closed on Sundays
Tabldot	Set price menu
Türk yemekleri	Turkish cuisine
Yemek listesi	Menu
Yerli içkiler	Drinks produced in Turkey

You may want to say

General phrases

Is there a cheap restaurant around here?
Yakında ucuz bir lokanta var mı?
yakuhnda ujuz bir lokanta varmuh

A (one) ... please
Bir ... lütfen
bir ... lewtfen

Another ... please
Bir ... daha lütfen
bir ... daha lewtfen

More ... please
Biraz daha ... lütfen
biraz daha ... lewtfen

For me
Bana
bana

For him/her
Ona
ona

For them
Onlara
onlara

This one, please
Bu lütfen
bu lewtfen

Two of these, please
Bundan iki tane lütfen
bundan iki ta:ne lewtfen

Do you have ...?
... var mı?
... varmuh

What is there to eat?
Ne yemek var?
ne yemek var

What is there for dessert?
Tatlı ne var?
tatluh ne var

What do you recommend?
Siz ne tavsiye edersiniz?
siz ne tavsi-ye edersiniz

Do you have any typical local dishes?
Bu bölgenin özel bir yemeği var mı?
bu bölgenin özel bir yeme:i varmuh

What's this?
Bu ne?
bu ne

How do you eat this?
Bu nasıl yenir?
bu nasuhl yenir

Cheers!
Şerefe!
sherefe

Enjoy your meal!
Afiyet olsun!
a:fi-yet olsun

Nothing else, thank you
**Başka bir şey istemez,
teşekkür ederim**
*bashka bir shey istemez
teshekkewr ederim*

Cafés and bars

A medium Turkish
coffee, please
Bir orta kahve lütfen
bir orta kahve lewtfen

A black coffee, please
Bir sütsüz neskahve lütfen
bir sewtsewz neskahve lewtfen

Two white coffees, please
İki sütlü neskahve lütfen
iki sütlü neskahve lewtfen

A tea with milk/lemon, please
Bir sütlü/limonlu çay lütfen
*bir sewtlew/limonlu chiy
lewtfen*

(Fizzy) mineral water, please
Maden suyu lütfen
ma:den suyu lewtfen

The bill, please
Hesap lütfen
hesap lewtfen

Where's the toilet?
Tuvalet nerede?
tuvalet nerede

A small bottle of (still) water
Bir küçük şişe su
bir kewchewk shishe su

A fizzy orange, please
Bir portakallı gazoz lütfen
bir portakalluh gazoz lütfen

What fruit juices do you
have?
Meyve suyu ne var?
meyve suyu ne var

An orange juice, please
Bir portakal suyu lütfen
bir portakal suyu lewtfen

A beer, please
Bir bira lütfen
bir bira lewtfen

A glass of red/white wine, please
Bir bardak kırmızı/beyaz şarap lütfen
bir bardak kuhrmuhzuh/ beyaz sharap lewtfen

A gin and tonic, please
Bir cin-tonik lütfen
bir jin tonik lewtfen

With ice
Buzlu
buzlu

What snacks do you have?
Çerez ne var?
cherez ne var

Some olives, please
Biraz zeytin lütfen
biraz zeytin lewtfen

Some crisps, please
Biraz cips lütfen
biraz jips lewtfen

A (large) portion of fried squid
Bir (büyük) porsiyon kalamar tava
bir (bewyewk) porsiyon kalamar tava

What sandwiches do you have?
Sandviç ne var?
sandvich ne var

An egg sandwich, please
Bir yumurtalı sandviç lütfen
bir yumurtaluh sandvich lewtfen

Two cheese sandwiches, please
İki peynirli sandviç lütfen
iki peynirli sandvich lewtfen

Do you have ice-cream?
Dondurma var mı?
dondurma varmuh

What flavours do you have?
Neli var?
neli var

A chocolate/vanilla/fruit ice, please
Çikolatalı /Vanilyalı/ Meyveli dondurma lütfen
chikolataluh/vanilyaluh/ meyveli dondurma lewtfen

A mixed ice, please
Bir karışık dondurma lütfen
bir karuhshuhk dondurma lewtfen

91

Booking a table

I'd like to reserve a table for two people
İki kişilik bir masa ayırtmak istiyorum
iki kishilik bir masa iyuhrtmak istiyorum

For eight o'clock
Saat sekiz için
saat sekiz ichin

For half past seven
tomorrow evening
Yarın akşam yedi buçuk için
*yaruhn aksham yedi buchuk
ichin*

I've booked a table
Bir masa ayırttım
bir masa iyuhrttuhm

The name is ...
İsim ...
isim ...

In restaurants

A table for four, please
Dört kişilik bir masa lütfen
dört kishilik bir masa lewtfen

Outside, please
Dışarda lütfen
duhsharda lewtfen

Waiter/waitress!
Garson!
garson

The menu, please
Liste lütfen
liste lewtfen

Do you have a set menu?
Tabldot var mı?
tabldot varmuh

Do you have vegetarian
dishes?
Etsiz yemek var mı?
etsiz yemek varmuh

I don't eat meat, fish or
chicken
**Ben et, balık, tavuk
yemiyorum**
*ben et, baluhk, tavuk
yemiyorum*

The set menu, please
Tabldot lütfen
tabldot lewtfen

For the first course ...
Ordövr olarak ...
ordövr olarak ...

First ...
Önce ...
önje

Lentil soup, please
Mercimek çorbası lütfen
merjimek chorbasuh lewtfen

Two mixed hors d'œuvres, please
İki karışık ordövr lütfen
iki karuhshuhk ordövr lewtfen

For the next course ...
Sonra ...
sonra ...

Lamb chop, please
Kuzu pirzola lütfen
kuzu pirzola lewtfen

Are vegetables included?
Sebze dahil mi?
sebze daċhilmi

What comes with it?
Yanında ne var?
yanuhnda ne var

Chips, please
Kızarmış patates lütfen
kuhzarmuhsh patates lewtfen

And a mixed salad
Ve bir karışık salata
ve bir karuhshuhk salata

For dessert ...
Tatlı olarak ...
tatluh olarak ...

Baklava, please
Baklava lütfen
baklava lewtfen

A peach, please
Bir şeftali lütfen
bir shefta:li lewtfen

Excuse me, where are my chips?
Affedersiniz, benim patates nerede?
affedersiniz benim patates nerede

More bread, please
Daha ekmek lütfen
daha ekmek lewtfen

More rice, please
Daha pilav lütfen
daha pilav lewtfen

A glass/bottle of water
Bir bardak/şişe su
bir bardak/shishe su

A bottle of red wine
Bir şişe kırmızı şarap
bir shishe kuhrmuhzuh sharap

A single measure of rakı
Bir tek rakı
bir tek rakuh

A half-bottle of rakı
Bir küçük şişe rakı
bir kewchewk shishe rakuh

A double vodka
Bir duble votka
bir duble votka

It's very good
Çok güzel
chok gewzel

It's delicious
Çok lezzetli
chok lezzetli

This is burnt
Bu yanmış
bu yanmuhsh

This isn't cooked
Bu pişmemiş
bu pishmemish

No, I ordered the chicken
Hayır, ben tavuk istedim
hayuhr ben tavuk istedim

The bill, please
Hesap lütfen
hesap lewtfen

Do you accept credit cards?
Kredi kartı alıyor musunuz?
kredi kartuh aluhyor musunuz

Do you accept travellers' cheques?
Seyahat çeki alıyor musunuz?
seyahat cheki aluhyor musunuz

Excuse me, there's a mistake here
Affedersiniz, bir yanlış var
affedersiniz bir yanluhsh var

You may hear

Cafés and Bars

Ne istersiniz?
ne istersiniz
What would you like?

Ne içersiniz?
ne ichersiniz
What would you like to drink?

Buzlu mu?
buzlumu
With ice?

Buz ister misiniz?
buz istermisiniz
Would you like some ice?

Büyük mü, küçük mü?
bewyewkmew kewchewkmew
Large or small?

Hangisini istersiniz?
hangisini istersiniz
Which do you prefer?

... var
... var
We have ...

Restaurants

Kaç kişisiniz?
kach kishisiniz
How many are you?

Kaç kişilik?
kach kishilik
For how many people?

Bir dakika lütfen
bir daki:ka lewtfen
Just a moment, please

Masa ayırttınız mı?
masa iyuhrttuhnuhzmuh
Have you booked a table?

Biraz bekliyeceksiniz
biraz bekliyejeksiniz
You'll have to wait a little

Biraz bekler misiniz?
biraz bekler misiniz
Would you mind waiting a
little?

Ne istersiniz?
ne istersiniz
What would you like?

Bir aperitif ister misiniz?
bir aperitif ister misiniz
Would you like an aperitif?

... tavsiye ederim
... tavsi-ye ederim
I would recommend ...

Ordövr olarak
ordövr olarak
For the first course

Önce ..., arkasından ...
önje ..., arkasuhndan ...
First ..., after that ...

İçki olarak?
ichki olarak
To drink?

Balık tava mı, ızgara mı?
baluhk tavamuh uhzgaramuh
Is the fish to be fried or
grilled?

**Biftek az pişmiş mi, çok
pişmiş mi olsun?**
*biftek az pishmishmi chok
pishmishmi olsun*
Would you like the steak
rare or well done?

Bitirdiniz mi?
bitirdiniz mi
Have you finished?

Tatlı ister misiniz?
tatluh ister misiniz
Would you like dessert?

Kahve ister misiniz?
kahve ister misiniz
Would you like coffee?

Başka bir şey?
bashka bir shey
Anything else?

MENU READER

General phrases

Akşam yemeği	Dinner
Alkollü içkiler	Alcoholic drinks
Balık	Fish
Bira	Beer
Çerez	Snacks
Çorbalar	Soups
Deniz mahsulleri	Sea-food
Et yemekleri	Meat dishes
Günün yemeği	Dish of the day
Hamur tatlıları	Pastries
Hesap	Bill
İçkiler	Drinks
KDV dahil	VAT included
Kahvaltı	Breakfast
Maden suyu	Mineral water
Meşrubat	Soft drinks
Meyve	Fruit
Meze	Starters, Hors d'œuvres
Mönü	Menu
Mutfak	Kitchen
Öğle yemeği	Lunch
Porsiyon	Portion
Rakı	Raki (aniseed-flavoured spirit)
Salata	Salad
Sandviç	Sandwich
Sebzeler	Vegetables
Servis dahil	Service included
Servis hariç	Service not included

Şarap, Şaraplar	Wine, Wines
Tabldot	Set menu
Tatlılar	Desserts
Tavuk	Chicken
Yarım porsiyon	Half portion
Yemek listesi	Menu
Zeytinyağlılar	Vegetables cooked in oil

Drinks

Alkol	Alcohol
Alkollü içkiler	Alcoholic drinks
Ayran	Yoghurt-based drink
Bardak	Glass
Bira	Beer
Brüt	Dry (*sparkling wine*)
Buz	Ice
Buzlu	Iced, with ice
Cin	Gin
Cin-tonik	Gin and tonic
Çay	Tea
Limonlu çay	Lemon tea
Sütlü çay	Tea with milk
Dömi-sek	Medium dry
Elma çayı	Apple tea
Fincan	Cup
Gazoz	Fizzy lemonade
Ihlamur	Linden blossom tea
Kahve	Coffee
Az şekerli	With a little sugar
Orta	Medium
Sade	Without sugar
Sütlü	With milk
Şekerli	Sweet

Kakao	Cocoa
Kanyak	Brandy
Likör	Liqueur
Kahve likörü	Mocha liqueur
Muz likörü	Banana liqueur
Nane likörü	Crème de menthe
Portakal likörü	Orange liqueur
Vişne likörü	Sour cherry liqueur
Limonata	Non-fizzy lemonade
Maden suyu	Mineral water
Meyve suyu	Fruit juice
Kayısı suyu	Apricot juice
Limon suyu	Lemon juice
Portakal suyu	Orange juice
Şeftali suyu	Peach juice
Üzüm suyu	Grape juice
Vişne suyu	Sour cherry juice
Soda	Soda water
Su	Water
Süt	Milk
Şampanya	Champagne
Şarap	Wine
Beyaz şarap	White wine
Kırmızı şarap	Red wine
Köpüklü şarap	Sparkling wine
Pembe/Roze şarap	Rosé wine
Sek	Dry
Şıra	Cider
Şişe	Bottle
Tonik	Tonic water
Vermut	Vermouth
Viski	Whisky
Votka	Vodka

Food

Acı	Hot (spicy); bitter
Adana kebap	**Şiş köfte** with chilli
Ahtapot	Octopus
Ahududu	Raspberry
Alabalık	Trout
Ananas	Pineapple
Ançüez	Anchovies
Antrkot	Entrecôte
Armut	Pear
Arnavut ciğeri	Fried liver cubes
Aşure	Sweet dish made of dried fruit and pulses
Ayçiçeği	Sunflower
Ayçiçeği yağı	Sunflower oil
Ayva	Quince
Badem	Almonds
Bakla	Broad beans
Bal	Honey
Balık	Fish
Bamya	Okra
Barbunya	Red mullet; type of bean
Beyaz peynir	White/feta cheese
Beyin	Brains
Bezelye	Peas
Biber	Pepper, capsicum
Biftek	Steak
Bisküvi	Biscuits
Bonfile	Fillet steak
Böbrek	Kidney
Börek	Savoury pastry/flan
Brüksel lahanası	Brussel sprouts
Buğulama	Poached
But	Leg
Buz	Ice

Cacık	Yoghurt with cucumber
Ceviz	Walnut
Ciğer	Liver
Çerkez tavuğu	Chicken with walnut purée
Çiğ	Raw
Çikolata	Chocolate
Çilek	Strawberry
Çoban salatası	Onion, tomato and cucumber salad
Çorba	Soup
Dana	Veal, beef
Defne	Bay leaves
Dereotu	Dill
Dil	Tongue
Dilbalığı	Sole
Dolma	Stuffed vine/cabbage leaves or peppers
Domates	Tomatoes
Dondurma	Ice-cream
Dut	Mulberry
Ekmek	Bread
Ekşi	Sour
Elma	Apple
Enginar	Globe artichoke
Erik	Plum
Et	Meat
Et suyu	Meat stock
Fasulye	Beans
Fesleğen	Basil
Fındık	Hazelnut
Fırın	Roast
Fileto	Fillet
Füme	Smoked
Greyfrut	Grapefruit
Güveç	Casserole
Hamur	Pastry
Hamur işi	Pastry dishes

Hardal	Mustard
Haşlama	Boiled; stewed
Havuç	Carrot
Helva	Halva, a Turkish sweet made with sesame
Hindi	Turkey
Hurma	Dates
Ispanak	Spinach
Istakoz	Lobster
Izgara	Grilled
İç pilav	Rice with nuts and raisins
İncir	Figs
İşkembe	Tripe
Jöle	Jelly
Kabak	Courgette; marrow; pumpkin
Kabak tatlısı	Stewed pumpkin in syrup
Kalamar	Squid
Kalkan	Turbot
Kara lahana	Red cabbage
Karanfil	Cloves
Karışık	Mixed
Karışık ızgara	Mixed grill
Karides	Prawns
Karnıbahar	Cauliflower
Karpuz	Water melon
Kaşar peyniri	Type of cheese similar to cheddar
Katı yumurta	Hard-boiled egg
Kavun	Melon
Kayısı	Apricot
Kaymak	Thick cream
Kaz	Goose
Kebap	Kebab: small pieces of grilled lamb

Çöp kebabı
Döner kebap
İskender kebap
Şiş kebap

} *see page 86 for types of kebab*

Kefal	Grey mullet
Kek	Cake
Kekik	Thyme
Kepek	Wholemeal
Kepek ekmeği	Wholemeal bread
Kerevit	Crayfish; scampi
Kereviz	Celery
Kestane	Chestnut
Ketçap	Ketchup
Kılıç balığı	Swordfish
Kıvırcık salata	Lettuce salad
Kıyma	Mince
Kızarmış	Fried; roasted
Kızarmış ekmek	Toast
Kızartma	Fried
Kimyon	Cumin
Kiraz	Cherry
Kokoreç	Grilled stuffed entrails
Komposto	Compote; stewed fruit
Konsome	Consommé; clear soup
Köfte	Burger, meatball
Çiğ köfte	minced lamb kneaded with wheat and served raw
Izgara köfte	grilled burgers
Şiş köfte	minced lamb in strips, grilled on skewers
Krem karamel	Crème caramel
Krema	Cream
Kuru üzüm	Raisins
Kuşkonmaz	Asparagus
Kuzu	Lamb
Lahana	Cabbage
Levrek	Sea bass
Limon	Lemon
Lokum	Turkish delight

Lüfer	Blue fish
Makarna	Spaghetti; pasta
Mandalina	Tangerine
Mantar	Mushrooms
Margarin	Margarine
Marmelat	Marmalade
Marul	Cos lettuce
Maydanoz	Parsley
Mayonez	Mayonnaise
Mercimek	Lentils
Meyve	Fruit
Meze	Starters
Mısır	Corn
Mısır yağı	Corn oil
Midye	Mussels
Muhallebi	Milk pudding
Muz	Banana
Nane	Mint
Nar	Pomegranate
Nohut	Chick pea
Omlet	Omelette
Ördek	Duck
Paça	Lamb's trotters
Palamut	Bonito (*similar to tuna fish*)
Pancar	Beetroot
Pasta	Gateau
Pastırma	Spiced cured beef
Patates	Potatoes
Patlıcan	Aubergine
Peynir	Cheese
Pırasa	Leeks
Pide	Pitta bread
Pilaki	Haricot beans in sauce
Pilav	Cooked rice
Piliç	Spring chicken

Pirinç	Rice
Pirzola	Chop
Pişmiş	Cooked
Piyaz	White bean salad
Püre	Mashed
Rakı	Aniseed-flavoured spirit
Reçel	Jam
Roka	Green salad rather like watercress
Rozbif	Roast beef
Sade	Without sugar; plain
Salam	Salami
Salata	Salad
Salatalık	Cucumber
Salça	Tomato sauce
Şamfıstığı	Pistachio nuts
Sandviç	Sandwich
Sardalya	Sardines
Sarmısak	Garlic
Sebze	Vegetables
Sıcak	Hot
Sigara böreği	Fried cheese-filled filo pastry
Sirke	Vinegar
Soğan	Onion
Soğuk	Cold
Som balığı	Salmon
Sos	Sauce
Sosis	Sausage
Sote	Sautéed
Söğüş	Cold meat; undressed salad
Sucuk	Spicy sausage
Süt	Milk
Süt tatlıları	Milk puddings
Sütlaç	Rice pudding
Şeftali	Peach
Şeker	Sugar

Şekerleme	Candied fruit
Şnitzel	Veal escalope
Tarator	Garlic and nut purée
Tarçın	Cinnamon
Tava	Fried
Tavuk	Chicken
Tavuk göğsü	Milk pudding
Taze	Fresh
Tereyağı	Butter
Ton balığı	Tuna fish
Torta	Tart
Tost	Toasted cheese sandwich
Tulum peyniri	Hard white cheese
Turp	Radish; turnip
Turşu	Pickles
Tuz	Salt
Un	Flour
Uskumru	Mackerel
Üzüm	Grapes
Vanilya	Vanilla
Vişne	Morello cherry
Yağ	Oil; butter; fat
Yengeç	Crayfish
Yer elması	Jerusalem artichoke
Yer fıstığı	Peanut
Yeşil salata	Lettuce salad
Yoğurt	Yoghurt
Yumurta	Egg
haşlama/katı	hard-boiled
rafadan	soft-boiled
yağda	fried
Zeytin	Olive
Zeytinyağı	Olive oil

SHOPPING

• Opening hours vary slightly, and some shops close for an hour or an hour and a half in the middle of the day. Most shops stay open until 7 p.m. in the summer and 6 p.m. in the winter, including Saturdays. In large towns and tourist centres, general grocers' shops (**bakkal**) and mini-supermarkets (**market**) stay open until 9.00 p.m. or so.

• There are a few chains of department stores with branches mainly in the big cities, where you'll also find large super-markets. Most shops, though, are small, individual ones.

• Many towns have street markets (**pazar**) once or twice a week. Some sell only fruit and vegetables and other foodstuffs, others sell almost anything. The **Kapalı Çarşı** (Grand Bazaar) in Istanbul is famous for its shops selling antiques, jewellery and precious metals, clothing and textiles, and leather goods. It's closed on Sundays. The other principal Istanbul bazaar, **Mısır Çarşısı** (the Egyptian Bazaar), sells mostly food and spices.

• Chemists (**eczane**) are generally open from 9.00 a.m. to 1 p.m. and 2 to 7 p.m. Mondays–Saturdays. There is always a **nöbetçi eczane** (duty chemist) open all night and on Sundays and public holidays. The address of the local duty chemist can be found displayed in the window of every chemist's shop. Toiletries and cosmetics are sold in a **parfümeri** rather than an **eczane**.

• Post offices are generally open from 8.30 a.m. to 12.30 p.m. and 1.30 to 5.30 p.m. Monday–Friday, and 8.30 to 12.30 on Saturdays. They are closed on Sundays. Ask for **postane**, but you will usually see the sign **PTT** outside a post office. Post-boxes are painted yellow and are also marked **PTT**.

● If you want to receive mail at a *poste restante*, have it addressed to **Postrestant** with the name of the locality or village you're staying in.

● To ask for something in a shop, all you need do is name it and add **lütfen** (please) – or just point and state how much/many you need.

● Bargaining is a usual practice when shopping for non-food items, particularly souvenirs, leather goods and antiques.

● Before you go shopping, try and make a list of what you need in Turkish. If you're looking for clothes or shoes, work out what size to ask for and other things like colour, material and so on. You can always write the details down and show them to the shop assistants.

● Shopkeepers and customers always exchange greetings and farewells, so check up on the correct phrases for the time of day (see All-purpose phrases, page 288).

You may see

Açık	Open
Açık artırma	Public auction
Alışveriş merkezi	Shopping mall
Alt kat	Lower ground floor
Antika	Antiques
Ayakkabıcı	Shoe shop, cobbler
Bakkal	Grocer
Balıkçı	Fishmonger
Berber	Barber
Bodrum	Basement
Butik	Boutique
Ceket	Jacket
Çarşı	Bazaar; shopping centre
Çekiniz	Pull
Çıkış	Exit

Çiçek	Flower
Çiçekçi	Florist
Deri	Leather, skin
Deri ceket	Leather jacket
Deri eşya	Leather goods
Eczane	Chemist's
Elbise	Clothes
Elektrikli eşya	Electrical goods
Eski	Old
Fiyat	Price
Giriş	Entrance
Giyim (eşyası)	Clothing
Göz doktoru	Eye specialist
Gözlükçü	Optician
Hamal	Porter
Hazır giyim eşyası	Ready-made clothes
Hediyelik eşya	Gifts, souvenirs
Hepsi	Everything
Her zaman	Always
İndirim	Reduction; sales
İstasyon	Station
İtiniz	Push
Kapalı	Closed
Kasa	Cashier
Kasap	Butcher
Kaset	Cassette
Kitapçı	Bookseller
Kitapevi	Bookshop
Konfeksiyon	Ready-to-wear
Kuaför	Hairdresser's
Kuru temizlemeci	Dry cleaner's
Kuru yemişçi	Dried fruit seller
Kuyumcu	Goldsmith's; jeweller's
Manav	Greengrocer
Mobilya	Furniture

Moda	Fashion
Mücevherci	Jeweller's
Müzikevi	Music shop
Nöbetçi eczane	Duty chemist's
Oyuncak	Toy
Oyuncakçı	Toy shop
Özel indirim	Special offer
Parfümeri	Perfumery
Pastane	Patisserie; smart café
Plak	Record
Plakçı	Record shop
Postane	Post Office
PTT	Post Office
Saat	Watch; clock
Saatçi	Watchmaker's
Self-servis	Self service
Soyunma odası	Changing room
Spor malzemesi	Sports equipment
Süpermarket	Supermarket
Tuhafiyeci	Haberdasher's
Yangın merdiveni	Fire escape
Yeni	New

You may want to say

General phrases

(See also Directions, page 25; Problems and complaints, page 147, Numbers, page 189 and inside front cover)

Where are the shops?
Dükkanlar nerede?
dewkkanlar nerede

Where's the chemist's?
Eczane nerede?
ejza:ne nerede

Is there a grocer's shop around here?
Buralarda bakkal var mı?
buralarda bakkal varmuh

Where can I buy batteries?
Pil nereden alabilirim?
pil nereden alabilirim

What time does the baker's open?
Fırın saat kaçta açılıyor?
fuhruhn saat kachta achuhluhyor

What time do you open in the morning?
Sabah saat kaçta açıyorsunuz?
sabah saat kachta achuhyorsunuz

What time do you close this evening?
Bu akşam saat kaçta kapatıyorsunuz?
bu aksham saat kachta kapatuhyorsunuz

Do you have ...?
... var mı ?
... varmuh

How much is it?
Kaç para?
kach para

How much does this cost?
Bu kaça?
bu kacha

How much do these cost?
Bunlar kaça?
bunlar kacha

I don't understand
Anlamıyorum
anlamuhyorum

Could you write it down please?
Lütfen yazar mısınız?
lewtfen yazar muhsuhnuhz

It's too expensive
Çok pahalı
chok pahaluh

Please reduce the price a bit
Biraz indirim yapın lütfen
biraz indirim yapuhn lewtfen

Haven't you got anything cheaper?
Daha ucuz bir şey yok mu?
daha ujuz bir shey yokmu

I don't have enough money
Yeter param yok
yeter param yok

Could you keep it for me?
Benim için saklar mısınız?
benim ichin saklar muhsuhnuhz

I'm just looking
Bakıyorum
bakuhyorum

This one, please
Bu lütfen
bu lewtfen

That one, please
Şu lütfen
shu lewtfen

Three of these
Bunlardan üç tane
bunlardan ewch ta:ne

Two of those
Şunlardan iki tane
shunlardan iki ta:ne

Not that one – this one
O değil, bu
o de:il bu

There's one in the window
Vitrinde bir tane var
vitrinde bir ta:ne var

That's fine
Tamam
tamam

Nothing else, thank you
Başka bir şey yok, teşekkür ederim
bashka birshey yok teshekkewr ederim

I'll take it
Alıyorum
aluhyorum

I'll think about it
Düşüneyim
dewshewneyim

Have you got a bag?
Torba var mı?
torba varmuh

Could you wrap it for me?
Sarar mısınız?
sarar muhsuhnuhz

With plenty of paper
Bol kağıtla
bol ka:uhtla

I'm taking it to England
İngiltere'ye götürüyorum
ingitereye götewrewyorum

It's a gift
Hediye
hediye

Where do I pay?
Parayı nereye ödeyeceğim?
pariyuh nereye ödeyece:im

Do you take credit cards?
Kredi kartı alıyor musunuz?
kredi kartuh aluhyor musunuz

Do you take travellers' cheques?
Seyahat çeki alıyor musunuz?
seyahat cheki aluhyor musunuz

I'm sorry, I don't have any change
Özür dilerim, bozuk param yok
özewr dilerim bozuk param yok

Could you give me a receipt?
Bir fatura verir misiniz?
bir fatura verir misiniz

Buying food and drink

A kilo of ...
Bir kilo ...
bir kilo...

A kilo of grapes, please
Bir kilo üzüm lütfen
bir kilo ewzewm lewtfen

Two kilos of oranges, please
İki kilo portakal lütfen
iki kilo portakal lewtfen

Half a kilo of tomatoes, please
Yarım kilo domates lütfen
yaruhm kilo domates lewtfen

A hundred grams of ...
Yüz gram ...
yewz gram ...

A hundred grams of olives, please
Yüz gram zeytin lütfen
yewz gram zeytin lewtfen

Two hundred grams of salami, please
İki yüz gram salam lütfen
iki yewz gram salam lewtfen

Sliced
Dilimli
dilimli

A little cheese, please
Biraz peynir lütfen
biraz peynir lewtfen

A packet of sausages, please
Bir paket sosis lütfen
bir paket sosis lewtfen

A bottle of white wine, please
Bir şişe beyaz şarap lütfen
bir shishe beyaz sharap lewtfen

Two cans of beer, please
İki teneke kutu bira lütfen
iki teneke kutu bira lewtfen

A bit of that, please
Şundan biraz lütfen
shundan biraz lewtfen

A bit more
Biraz daha
biraz daha

A bit less
Daha az
daha az

What's this?
Bu ne?
bu ne

What's in this?
Bunda ne var?
bunda ne var

Can I try it?
Tadına bakabilir miyim?
taduhna bakabilir mi-yim

At the chemist's

Aspirins, please
Aspirin lütfen
aspirin lewtfen

Plasters, please
Flaster lütfen
flaster lewtfen

Do you have something for ...?
... için bir şey var mı?
... ichin bir shey varmuh

Do you have something for diarrhoea?
Diyare için bir şey var mı?
diyare ichin bir shey varmuh

Do you have something for insect bites?
Böcek ısırığı için bir şey var mı?
böjek uhsuhruh:uh ichin bir shey varmuh

Do you have something for period pains?
Aybaşı sancısı için bir şey var mı?
iybashuh sanjuhsuh ichin bir shey varmuh

Buying clothes and shoes

I'd like a skirt
Bir etek istiyorum
bir etek istiyorum

I'd like a shirt/blouse
Bir gömlek istiyorum
bir gömlek istiyorum

I'd like a pair of sandals
Sandalet istiyorum
sandalet istiyorum

I'd like a pair of shoes
Ayakkabı istiyorum
iyakkabuh istiyorum

Size 40
Kırk numara
kuhrk numara

Can I try it on?
Giyebilir miyim?
giyebilir mi-yim

Is there a mirror?
Ayna var mı?
iyna var muh

I like it/them
Beğendim
be:endim

I don't like it/them
Beğenmedim
be:enmedim

It's/They're too small
Çok küçük
chok kewchewk

I don't like the colour
Rengini beğenmedim
rengini be:enmedim

Have you got a smaller size?
Daha küçüğü var mı?
daha kewchew:ew varmuh

Do you have it in other colours?
Başka renk var mı?
bashka renk varmuh

Have you got a bigger size?
Daha büyüğü var mı?
daha bewyew:ew varmuh

It's/They're too big
Çok büyük
chok bewyewk

Miscellaneous

Five stamps for England, please
İngiltere için beş pul lütfen
ingiltere ichin besh pul lewtfen

A film like this, please
Bunun gibi bir film lütfen
bunun gibi bir film lewtfen

Three postcards, please
Üç kart lütfen
ewch kart lewtfen

A film for this camera
Bu fotoğraf makinesi için bir film
bu foto:raf makinesi ichin bir film

Matches, please
Kibrit lütfen
kibrit lewtfen

Do you have any English newspapers?
İngiliz gazetesi var mı?
ingiliz gazetesi varmuh

You may hear

Buyurun
buyurun
Yes please?

(Size) yardım edebilir miyim?
(size) yarduhm edebilir mi-yim
Can I help you?

Ne istiyorsunuz?
ne istiyorsunuz
What do you want?

Ne kadar istiyorsunuz?
ne kadar istiyorsunuz
How much do you want?

Kaç tane istiyorsunuz?
kach ta:ne istiyorsunuz
How many do you want?

Tamam mı?
tamam muh
Is that OK?

Başka bir şey?
bashka bir shey
Anything else?

Özür dilerim, kalmadı
özewr dilerim kalmaduh
I'm sorry, we're sold out

Özür dilerim, şimdi kapalıyız
özewr dilerim shimdi kapaluhyuhz
I'm sorry, we're closed now

Sarayım mı?
sariyuhm muh
Shall I wrap it?

Lütfen kasaya ödeyin
lewtfen kasiya ödeyin
Please pay at the cash desk

Bozuk var mı?
bozuk varmuh
Do you have any change?

Bozuk yok mu?
bozuk yokmu
Don't you have any change?

Reçete lazım
rechete la:zuhm
You need a prescription

Kaç bedensiniz?
kach bedensiniz
What size are you?

Nasıl ...?
nasuhl ...
What sort of ...?

Nasıl bir film istiyorsunuz?
nasuhl bir film istiyorsunuz
What sort of film do you want?

Nasıl bir fotoğraf makinesi için?
nasuhl bir foto:raf makinesi ichin
What sort of camera is it for?

115

BUSINESS TRIPS

● You'll probably be using English for doing business, or you'll have an interpreter to help you, but a few Turkish phrases can be helpful, especially if you have to make an appointment or leave a message.

● You may find yourself addressed as **Beyefendi** (Sir) or **Hanımefendi** (Madam), which are very formal expressions – but you don't have to use these yourself. You should address people you meet as **Sayın** followed by their surname: this goes for both men and women, e.g. **Sayın Özdemir**. Once you get to know a business associate, though, it would be too formal to go on using **Sayın**. You should call him by his first name followed by **Bey** if he is a man, or by her first name followed by **Hanım** if she's a woman, e.g. **Süleyman Bey**, **Ayşe Hanım**.

You may see

Asansör	Lift
A.Ş. (Anonim Şirket)	Co. Ltd., PLC
Birinci kat	First floor
Bozuk	Out of order
Çıkış	Exit
Giriş	Entrance
Girmek yasaktır	Entry prohibited
Görevliler dışında kimse giremez	No entry to unauthorised persons
İkinci kat	Second floor
Merdiven	Stairs
Sigara içilmez	No smoking
Üçüncü kat	Third floor
Yangın merdiveni	Fire escape
Zemin kat	Ground floor

You may want to say

(See also Days, months, dates, page 170; Time, page 173)

Mr Genç, please
Sayın Genç lütfen
siyuhn gench lewtfen

The manager, please
Müdür lütfen
mewdewr lewtfen

My name is ...
İsmim ...
ismim ...

My company is ...
Şirketim ...
shirketim ...

I have an appointment
with Mr Ali Özver
**Sayın Ali Özver'le
randevum var**
*siyuhn ali özverle randevum
var*

I don't have an appointment
Randevum yok
randevum yok

I'd like to make an
appointment with Miss/
Mrs Kızılca
**Sayın Kızılca'dan bir
randevu istiyorum**
*siyuhn kuhzuhljadan bir
randevu istiyorum*

I'm free this afternoon (at
4 o'clock)
**Bugün öğleden sonra (saat
dörtte) boşum**
*bugewn ö:leden sonra (saat
dörtte) boshum*

I'd like to talk to the
export manager
**İhracat müdürü ile
görüşmek istiyorum**
*ihra:jat mewdewrew ile
görewshmek istiyorum*

What's his/her name?
İsmi ne?
ismi ne

When will he/she be back?
Ne zaman döner?
ne zaman döner

Can I leave a message?
Mesaj bırakabilir miyim?
mesazh buhrakabilir mi-yim

Could you ask him/her to
call me?
Beni aramasını söyler misiniz?
*beni aramasuhnuh
söylermisiniz*

My telephone number is ...
Telefon numaram ...
telefon numaram ...

117

I'm staying at the Gezi Hotel
Gezi Otelinde kalıyorum
gezi otelinde kaluhyorum

Where's his/her office?
Bürosu nerede?
bewrosu nerede

I've come for the exhibition
Sergi için geldim
sergi ichin geldim

I've come for the fair
Fuar için geldim
fuar ichin geldim

I've come for the conference
Konferans için geldim
konferans ichin geldim

I have to make a phone call (to England)
(İngiltere'ye) telefon etmem lazım
(ingiltereye) telefon etmem la:zuhm

I have to send a telex
Bir teleks göndermem lazım
bir teleks göndermem la:zuhm

I have to send this by fax
Bunu faksla göndermem lazım
bunu faksla göndermem la:zuhm

I'd like to send this by post
Bunu postayla göndermek istiyorum
bunu postiyla göndermek istiyorum

I'd like to send this by courier
Bunu kuryeyle göndermek istiyorum
bunu kuryeyle göndermek istiyorum

I need someone to type a letter for me
Bana bir mektup daktilo edecek biri lazım
bana bir mektup daktilo edejek biri la:zuhm

I need a photocopy of this
Bunun bir fotokopisi lazım
bunun bir fotokopisi la:zuhm

I need an interpreter
Bana bir tercüman lazım
bana bir terjewman la:zuhm

You may hear

İsminiz lütfen
isminiz lewtfen
Your name, please

İsminiz nedir?
isminiz nedir
What's your name?

Şirketinizin ismi lütfen
shirketinizin ismi lewtfen
The name of your
company, please

Randevunuz var mı?
randevunuz varmuh
Do you have an
appointment?

Kartvizitiniz var mı?
kartvizitiniz varmuh
Do you have a card?

Sizi bekliyor mu?
sizi bekliyormu
Is he/she expecting you?

Bir dakika (bekleyin) lütfen
bir dakika (bekleyin) lewtfen
(Wait) one moment, please

Geldiğinizi haber vereyim
geldi:inizi haber vereyim
I'll tell him/her you've arrived

Hemen geliyor
hemen geliyor
He/she's just coming

Oturun lütfen
oturun lewtfen
Sit down, please

Oturmaz mısınız?
oturmaz muhsuhnuhz
Wouldn't you like to sit
down?

Bir şey içer misiniz?
bir shey icher misiniz
Would you like something
to drink?

Buyurun lütfen
buyurun lewtfen
Please go in

Şöyle buyurun lütfen
shöyle buyurun lewtfen
Come this way, please

Sayın Genç burada değil
siyuhn gench burada de:il
Mr/Mrs/Miss Genç is not
here

Sayın Atalar seyahatte
siyuhn atalar seyahatte
Mr/Mrs/Miss Atalar is on
a journey

119

Sayın Yorulmaz yarımda dönecek
siyuhn yorulmaz yaruhmda dönejek
Mr/Mrs/Miss Yorulmaz will be back at 12.30

Yarım saate kadar
yaruhm saate kadar
In half an hour

Asansörle sekizinci kata çıkın
asansörle sekizinji kata chuhkuhn
Take the lift to the eighth floor

Koridoru geçin
koridoru gechin
Go along the corridor

Solda üçüncü oda
solda ewchewnjew oda
Third room on the left

Sağda ikinci kapı
sa:da ikinji kapuh
Second door on the right

Sağda/Solda
sa:da/solda
On the right/On the left

Dört yüz yirmi numaralı oda
dört yewz yirmi numaraluh oda
Room number 420

Girin!/Buyurun!
girin/buyurun
Come in!

SIGHTSEEING

● The Turkish Tourist Office in London (address, page 187) and local tourist offices in Turkey can supply information about sights worth seeing and about sightseeing tours by coach and with English-speaking guides – which are available in Istanbul and tourist areas.

● Opening hours vary for historic buildings, archaeological sites, museums, galleries. Most are shut on Mondays or Tuesdays – check with the local tourist office.

● Mosques are open for most of the day, but you should avoid going in during prayer times – it'll be clear when these are about to start, because you'll hear the call to prayer recited from the minaret (the thin tower beside the mosque), usually through a loudspeaker, and a lot of worshippers will be entering the building. If you do find yourself in a mosque during prayer-time, stand or kneel quietly at the back until the prayers are over. Because worshippers in mosques put their heads on the carpet during prayer, the mosque floor has to be kept scrupulously clean; you must not go in with your shoes on. You should take off your shoes and leave them on the racks provided – watch other people going in to see what they do. Don't go into a mosque wearing shorts, sleeveless dresses or very short skirts; women will be expected to cover their heads. You shouldn't take photographs inside a mosque.

You may see

Açık	Open
Çimenlere basmayınız	Don't walk on the grass
Girmek yasaktır	Entry prohibited
Kapalı	Closed
Lütfen el sürmeyiniz	Please don't touch
Milli park	National park
Özel	Private
Rehberli turlar	Guided tours
Tamirat nedeniyle kapalı	Closed for repairs
Ziyaret saatleri	Visiting hours

You may want to say

(See Time, page 173)

When is the museum open?
Müze ne zaman açık?
mewze ne zaman achuhk

What time is the palace open?
Saray saat kaçta açılıyor?
sariy saat kachta achuhluhyor

What time does the museum close?
Müze saat kaçta kapanıyor?
mewze saat kachta kapanuhyor

Is it open on Mondays?
Pazartesi günleri açık mı?
pazartesi gewnleri achuhk muh

Can we go into the mosque?
Camiye girebilir miyiz?
ja:miye girebilir mi-yiz

Is it open to the public?
Halka açık mı?
halka achuhkmuh

Visiting places

One/two, please
Bir/İki lütfen
bir/iki lewtfen

Two adults and one child
İki büyük, bir çocuk
iki bewyewk bir chojuk

Are there reductions for children?
Çocuklara indirim var mı?
chojuklara indirim varmuh

For students
Öğrencilere
ö:rencilere

For pensioners
Emeklilere
emeklilere

For the disabled
Sakatlara
sakatlara

For groups
Gruplara
gruplara

Are there guided tours (in English)?
(İngilizce) rehberli turlar var mı?
(ingilizce) rehberli turlar varmuh

Can I take photos?
Fotoğraf çekebilir miyim?
foto:raf chekebilir mi-yim

Would you mind taking a photo of me/us, please?
Fotoğrafımı/Fotoğrafımızı çeker misiniz?
foto:rafuhmuh/ foto:rafuhmuhzuh cheker misiniz

When was this built?
Bu ne zaman yapılmış?
bu ne zaman yapuhlmuhsh

Who painted that picture?
O resmi kim yapmış?
o resmi kim yapmuhsh

In what year?
Hangi yılda?
hangi yuhlda

In what century?
Hangi yüzyılda?
hangi yewzyuhlda

What's this flower called?
Bu çiçeğin adı ne?
bu chiche:in aduh ne

What's this bird called?
Bu kuşun adı ne?
bu kushun aduh ne

Is there a picnic area (in the park)?
(Parkta) piknik alanı var mı?
(parkta) piknik alanuh varmuh

Sightseeing excursions

What excursions are there?
Hangi turlar var?
hangi turlar var

Are there any excursions to
Göreme?
Göreme'ye tur var mı?
göremeye tur varmuh

What time does it leave?
Saat kaçta hareket ediyor?
saat kachta hareket ediyor

Where does it leave from?
Nereden hareket ediyor?
nereden hareket ediyor

How long does it last?
Ne kadar sürüyor?
ne kadar sewrewyor

What time does it end?
Saat kaçta bitiyor?
saat kachta bitiyor

What time does it start back?
Saat kaçta geri dönüyor?
saat kachta geri dönewyor

Does the guide speak
English?
Rehber İngilizce biliyor mu?
rehber ingilizje biliyormu

How much is it?
Kaç para?
kach para

You may hear

Müze Pazartesi hariç her gün açık
mewze pazartesi ha:rich her gewn achuhk
The museum is open every day except Monday

Pazartesi günleri kapalı
pazartesi gewnleri kapaluh
It's closed on Mondays

Cami onaltıncı yüzyılda yapılmış
ja:mi onaltuhnjuh yewzyuhlda yapuhlmuhsh
The mosque was built in the sixteenth century

Bu tablo Hikmet Onat'ın
bu tablo hikmet onatuhn
This painting is by Hikmet Onat

Her Salı ve Perşembe gezi var
her saluh ve pershembe gezi var
There are excursions every Tuesday and Thursday

Otobüs saat onda Taksim meydanından kalkıyor
otobews saat onda taksim meydanuhndan kalkuhyor
The bus leaves at 10 o'clock from Taksim Square

ENTERTAINMENT

● Football is the most popular spectator sport in Turkey. Most professional fixtures take place on Sundays.

● Evening performances at cinemas and theatres and most concerts start mainly around 9 p.m.

● Turkey has a thriving film industry, but many American, British and other foreign films are shown in Turkish cinemas. Most of them are subtitled (**altyazılı**), but some are dubbed (**dublaj**).

● Turkish pop music has a very strong following and can be heard in cafés and restaurants all over the country – so can traditional Turkish oriental music, which expresses a wide variety of moods, such as unrequited love, happiness and social injustice.

You may see

Ara	Interval
Balkon	Balcony, circle
Bilet yok	Sold out
Büfe	Buffet
Canlı yayın	Live transmission
Çıkış	Exit
Giriş	Entrance
Hipodrom	Race course
Kapı	Door
Koltuk	Stalls
Konser	Concert
Konser salonu	Concert hall
Koşu	Race

Maç	Match (sports)
Matine	Matinée
Opera	Opera
Orijinal	In original language with subtitles
Orkestra	Orchestra
Renkli	In colour
Sahne	Stage
Seans	Performance (cinema)
Sıra	Row
Sinema	Cinema
Sirk	Circus
Stadyum	Stadium
Sürekli gösteri	Continuous performance
Tiyatro	Theatre
Tuvalet	Toilets
Vestiyer	Cloakroom
Yer numarası	Seat number

You may want to say

What's on

(See Time, page 173)

What is there to do in the evenings?
Akşamları yapacak ne var?
akshamlaruh yapajak ne var

Is there a disco around here?
Yakında bir disko var mı?
yakuhnda bir disko varmuh

Is there music in this restaurant?
Bu lokantada müzik var mı?
bu lokantada mewzik varmuh

Is there any entertainment for children?
Çocuklar için bir eğlence var mı?
chojuklar ichin bir e:lenje varmuh

What's on tonight?
Bu akşam ne oynuyor?
bu aksham ne oynuyor

What's on tomorrow?
Yarın ne oynuyor?
yaruhn ne oynuyor

At the cinema
Sinemada
sinemada

At the theatre
Tiyatroda
tiyatroda

Who's playing? (*team sport*)
Kim oynuyor?
kim oynuyor

Who's playing? (*music*)
Kim çalıyor?
kim chaluhyor

Who's singing this song?
Bu şarkıyı kim söylüyor?
bu sharkuhyuh kim söylewyor

Does the film have subtitles?
Film altyazılı mı?
film altyazuhluhmuh

Is there a football match
on Sunday?
**Pazar günü bir futbol maçı
var mı?**
*pazar gewnew bir futbol
machuh varmuh*

What time does the concert
start?
Konser saat kaçta başlıyor?
konser saat kachta bashluhyor

How long does it last?
Ne kadar sürüyor?
ne kadar sewrewyor

What time does it end?
Saat kaçta bitiyor?
saat kachta bitiyor

Tickets

Where can I get tickets?
Bilet nereden alabilirim?
bilet nereden alabilirim

Could you get me tickets
for the football match?
**Futbol maçı için bana bilet
alır mısınız?**
*futbol machuh ichin bana
bilet aluhr muhsuhnuhz*

For the concert
Konser için
konser ichin

For the cinema
Sinema için
sinema ichin

Two, please
İki lütfen
iki lewtfen

Two tickets for this evening, please
Bu akşam için iki bilet lütfen
bu aksham ichin iki bilet lewtfen

Are there any seats left for Saturday?
Cumartesi için yer var mı?
jumartesi ichin yer varmuh

I'd like to book two seats
İki kişilik yer ayırtmak istiyorum
iki kishilik yer iyuhrtmak istiyorum

For Friday
Cuma için
juma ichin

In the stalls
Koltuk
koltuk

In the balcony
Balkon
balkon

How much is a ticket?
Bir bilet kaç para?
bir bilet kach para

Do you have anything cheaper?
Daha ucuzu var mı?
daha ujuzu varmuh

That's fine
Tamam
tamam

At the show/game

Where is this, please?
(*showing your ticket*)
Bu nerede?
bu nerede

Where is the cloakroom?
Vestiyer nerede?
vestiyer nerede

Where is the buffet?
Büfe nerede?
bewfe nerede

Where is the toilet?
Tuvalet nerede?
tuvalet nerede

A programme, please
Bir program lütfen
bir program lewtfen

Where can I get a programme?
Bir program nereden alabilirim?
bir program nereden alabilirim

Is there an interval?
Ara var mı?
ara varmuh

You may hear

Biletleri burada otelden alabilirsiniz
biletleri burada otelden alabilirsiniz
You can buy the tickets here in the hotel

Konser salonunda
konser salonunda
At the concert hall

Stadyumda
stadyumda
At the stadium

Saat dokuzda başlıyor
saat dokuzda bashluhyor
It begins at nine o'clock

İki saat on beş dakika sürüyor
iki saat on besh daki:ka sewrewyor
It lasts two and a quarter hours

Saat on bir buçukta bitiyor
saat on bir buchukta bitiyor
It ends at half past eleven

On beş dakikalık bir ara var
on besh dakikaluhk bir ara var
There's a 15-minute interval

Ne zaman için?
ne zaman ichin
For when?

Balkon mu, koltuk mu?
balkonmu koltukmu
Circle or stalls?

Burada iki koltuk var
burada iki koltuk var
There are two here in the stalls (*indicating on seating plan*)

Maalesef hiç bilet kalmadı
maalesef hich bilet kalmaduh
Unfortunately there are no seats left

Biletinizi görebilir miyim?
biletinizi görebilir mi-yim
May I see your ticket?

SPORTS AND ACTIVITIES

● Turkey provides good facilities for water sports, winter sports and shooting. The Turkish Tourist Office or specialist travel agents can provide information about locations in Turkey.

● Beaches close to big cities like Istanbul and Izmir are polluted, but the Mediterranean and Aegean coasts have excellent beaches. The Sea of Marmara and the Black Sea also have good beaches, but the season is shorter there. The eastern end of the Black Sea coast is one of the most spectacular parts of the country, but it has a very heavy rainfall.

● You may see warning signs at the beach, such as **Denize girmek tehlikeli ve yasaktır** (It is dangerous and prohibited to go in the sea), and **Yüzmek tehlikelidir** (Swimming is dangerous). At some beaches, a line of buoys parallel to the shore indicates where the water gets deep. Most beaches don't have lifeguards, so you should always be on your guard when in the sea.

You may see

Atış sahası	Shooting range
Avlanmak yasaktır	Hunting prohibited
Balık tutmak yasaktır	Fishing prohibited
Denize girmek tehlikeli ve yasaktır	It is dangerous and prohibited to go in the sea
Kapalı yüzme havuzu	Indoor swimming pool
Kiralık	For hire
Kiralık sandal	Boats for hire
Plaj	Beach

Şemsiye	Umbrella/sunshade
Tehlike	Danger
Tenis kortu	Tennis court
Yelken kulübü	Yacht club
Yüzme havuzu	Swimming pool
Yüzmek tehlikelidir	Swimming is dangerous

You may want to say

General phrases

Can I hire a bike?
Bisiklet kiralayabilir miyim?
bisiklet kira:liyabilir mi-yim

Can I go fishing?
**Balık tutmaya gidebilir
 miyim?**
*baluhk tutmiya gidebilir
 mi-yim*

Can I go horse-riding?
Ata binebilir miyim?
ata binebilir mi-yim

Where can I play tennis?
Nerede tenis oynayabilirim?
nerede tenis oyniyabilirim

Where can I swim?
Nerede yüzebilirim?
nerede yewzebilirim

I don't know how to
 water-ski
**Su kayağı yapmayı
 bilmiyorum**
*su kiya:uh yapmiyuh
 bilmiyorum*

Do you give lessons?
Ders veriyor musunuz?
ders veriyor musunuz

I'm a beginner
Ben yeni başlıyorum
ben yeni bashluhyorum

I'm quite experienced
Oldukça tecrübeliyim
oldukcha tejrewbeliyim

How much is it per hour?
Saati kaç para?
saati kach para

How much is it for the
 whole day?
Bütün bir günlüğü kaç para?
*bewtewn bir gewnlew:ew
 kach para*

Is there a reduction for children?
Çocuklar için indirim var mı?
chojuklar ichin indirim varmuh

Can I hire a boat?
Bir sandal kiralayabilir miyim?
bir sandal kira:liyabilir miyim

Can I hire equipment?
Malzeme kiralayabilir miyim?
malzeme kira:liyabilir mi-yim

Can I hire rackets?
Raket kiralayabilir miyim?
raket kira:liyabilir mi-yim

Is it necessary to be a member?
Üye olmak şart mı?
ewye olmak shartmuh

Beach and pool

Can I swim here?
Burada yüzebilir miyim?
burada yewzebilir mi-yim

Can I swim in the lake?
Gölde yüzebilir miyim?
gölde yewzebilir mi-yim

Is it dangerous?
Tehlikeli mi?
tehlikelimi

Is it safe for children?
Çocuklar için güvenli mi?
chojuklar ichin gewvenlimi

Is it deep?
Derin mi?
derinmi

Is it clean?
Temiz mi?
temizmi

You may hear

Su kayağı yapmayı biliyor musunuz?
su kiya:uh yapmayuh biliyor musunuz
Do you know how to water-ski?

Sörf yapmayı biliyor musunuz?
sörf yapmiyuh biliyor musunuz
Do you know how to wind-surf?

Saati ... lira
saati ... lira
It's ... liras per hour

... lira deposit vermeniz lazım
... lira depozit vermeniz la:zuhm
You have to pay a deposit of ... liras

Maalesef doluyuz
maalesef doluyuz
Unfortunately we're booked up

Daha sonra gelin lütfen
daha sonra gelin lewtfen
Please come back later

Kaç numara giyiyorsunuz?
kach numara giyiyorsunuz
What size do you wear?

Üyelik kartı için bir fotoğraf lazım
ewyelik kartuh ichin bir foto:raf la:zuhm
You need a photograph for the membership card

HEALTH

Medical details – to show to a doctor

(*Tick boxes or fill in details*)

	Self Kendiniz	Other members of family/party Beraberinizdekiler		
Blood group **Kan grubu**				
Asthmatic **Astımlı**				
Blind **Kör**				
Deaf **Sağır**				
Diabetic **Diabetli**				
Epileptic **Saralı**				
Handicapped **Sakat**				
Heart condition **Kalp rahatsızlığı**				
High blood pressure **Yüksek tansiyon**				
Pregnant **Hamile**				

Allergic to **Alerjik oldukları**			
Antibiotics **Antibiyotikler**			
Penicillin **Penisilin**			
Cortisone **Kortizon**			

Medicines **Alınan ilaçlar**

Self **Kendi** _____

Others **Diğerleri** _____

• Your local Department of Health office can provide information about medical care abroad and vaccinations which may be necessary. It is advisable to take out medical insurance before you travel.

• In Turkey, chemists can often give medical advice and basic first aid. They can provide certain medicines without a prescription.

• If you need an ambulance, call the emergency phone number 077.

• To indicate where the pain is, simply point and say **Burası ağrıyor** (it hurts here). Otherwise, you can look up the Turkish for the appropriate part of the body (page 145) and say 'my ... hurts'. To do this, add an *uhm* sound to the word, e.g. 'stomach' is **mide**; 'my stomach' is **midem**. See Basic grammar, page 155, for more on how to say 'my', 'his', 'her', etc.

You may see

Acil servis	Emergency service
Dahilen kullanılır	To be taken internally
Diş doktoru	Dentist
Diş tabibi	Dentist
Doktor	Doctor
Doktorun talimatına göre	According to the doctor's instructions
Dozaj	Dosage
Günde üç kere	Three times a day
Haricen kullanılır	For external use only
Hastane	Hospital
İlk yardım	First aid
İlk yardım merkezi	First aid post
Kullanım şekli	Instructions for use

Kullanmadan önce çalkalayınız	Shake before use
Muayene saatleri	Surgery hours
Poliklinik	Clinic
Sağlık ocağı	Basic medical care centre
Yemeklerden önce	Before meals
Yemeklerden sonra	After meals
Zehir	Poison
Zehirli madde	Poisonous substance

At the doctor's

You may want to say

I need a doctor
Bir doktor lazım
bir doktor la:zuhm

Please call a doctor
Doktor çağırın lütfen
doktor cha:uhruhn lewtfen

Urgently
Acele
ajele

Quickly
Çabuk
chabuk

Is there anyone who speaks
English?
İngilizce bilen var mı?
ingilizje bilen varmuh

Can I make an appointment?
Bir randevu alabilir miyim?
bir randevu alabilir mi-yim

It's my husband/wife
Eşim
eshim

It's my friend
Arkadaşım
arkadashuhm

It's my son
Oğlum
o:lum

It's my daughter
Kızım
kuhzuhm

How much will it cost?
Kaç para tutar?
kach para tutar

Your symptoms

I'm not well
İyi değilim
i-yi de:ilim

I feel awful
Çok kötüyüm
chok kötewyewm

It hurts here
Burası ağrıyor
burasuh a:ruhyor

My stomach hurts
Midem ağrıyor
midem a:ruhyor

My arm hurts
Kolum ağrıyor
kolum a:ruhyor

My feet hurt
Ayaklarım ağrıyor
iyaklaruhm a:ruhyor

My legs hurt
Bacaklarım ağrıyor
bajaklaruhm a:ruhyor

My chest hurts
Göğsüm ağrıyor
gö:sewm a:ruhyor

I have a headache
Başım ağrıyor
bashuhm a:ruhyor

I have a sore throat
Boğazım ağrıyor
bo:azuhm a:ruhyor

Someone else's symptoms

He/she feels unwell
İyi değil
i-yi de:il

He/she feels awful
Çok kötü
chok kötew

His/her stomach hurts
Midesi ağrıyor
midesi a:ruhyor

His/her arm hurts
Kolu ağrıyor
kolu a:ruhyor

His/her feet hurt
Ayakları ağrıyor
iyaklaruh a:ruhyor

His/her legs hurt
Bacakları ağrıyor
bajaklaruh a:ruhyor

His/her chest hurts
Göğsü ağrıyor
gö:sew a:ruhyor

He/she has a headache
Başı ağrıyor
bashuh a:ruhyor

He/she has a sore throat
Boğazı ağrıyor
bo:azuh a:ruhyor

He/she is unconscious
Kendini kaybetti
kendini kiybetti

He/she has fainted
Bayıldı
biyuhlduh

I have a temperature
Ateşim var
ateshim var

He/she has a temperature
Ateşi var
ateshi var

I have diarrhoea
Diyare oldum
di-yare oldum

He/she has diarrhoea
Diyare oldu
di-yare oldu

I feel dizzy
Başım dönüyor
bashuhm dönewyor

He/she is dizzy
Başı dönüyor
bashuh dönewyor

I feel sick
Midem bulanıyor
midem bulanuhyor

He/she feels sick
Midesi bulanıyor
midesi bulanuhyor

I've been sick
Kustum
kustum

He/she's been sick
Kustu
kustu

I can't sleep
Uyuyamıyorum
uyuyamuhyorum

He/she can't sleep
Uyuyamıyor
uyuyamuhyor

I can't breathe
Nefes alamıyorum
nefes alamuhyorum

He/she can't breathe
Nefes alamıyor
nefes alamuhyor

I can't move it
Oynatamıyorum
oynatamuhyorum

He/she can't move it
Oynatamıyor
oynatamuhyor

... is bleeding
... kanıyor
... kanuhyor

... is bleeding
... kanıyor
... kanuhyor

My nose is bleeding
Burnum kanıyor
burnum kanuhyor

His/her nose is bleeding
Burnu kanıyor
burnu kanuhyor

It's my arm
Kolum
kolum

It's his/her arm
Kolu
kolu

It's my leg
Bacağım
baja:uhm

It's his/her leg
Bacağı
baja:uh

It's broken
Kırıldı
kuhruhlduh

It's sprained
Burkuldu
burkuldu

I've sprained my ankle
Bileğim burkuldu
bile:im burkuldu

He/she has sprained his/her ankle
Bileği burkuldu
bile:i burkuldu

I've cut ...
... kestim
... kestim

He/she has cut ...
... kesti
... kesti

I've cut my finger
Parmağımı kestim
parma:uhmuh kestim

He/she has cut his/her finger
Parmağını kesti
parma:uhnuh kesti

I've burnt ...
... yandı
... yanduh

He/she has burnt ...
... yandı
... yanduh

I've burnt my hands
Ellerim yandı
ellerim yanduh

He/she has burnt his/her
hands
Elleri yandı
elleri yanduh

I've been stung by an insect
Beni böcek soktu
beni böjek soktu

He/she has been stung by
an insect
Onu böcek soktu
onu böjek soktu

I've been bitten by a dog
Beni köpek ısırdı
beni köpek uhsuhrduh

He/she has been bitten by
a dog
Onu köpek ısırdı
onu köpek uhsuhrduh

You may hear

Ne oldu
ne oldu
What happened?

Neresi ağrıyor?
neresi a:ruhyor
Where does it hurt?

Burası ağrıyor mu?
burasuh a:ruhyormu
Does it hurt here?

Çok mu, az mı?
chokmu azmuh
A lot or a little?

Ne zamandan beri böyle?
ne zamandan beri böyle
How long has it been like
this?

Kaç yaşındasınız?
kach yashuhndasuhnuhz
How old are you?

Kaç yaşında?
kach yashuhnda
How old is he/she?

Ağzınızı açın
a:zuhnuhzuh achuhn
Open your mouth

Öksürün!
öksewrewn
Cough!

Derin nefes alın
derin nefes aluhn
Take a deep breath

Soyunun
soyunun
Get undressed

Şuraya uzanın
shuriya uzanuhn
Lie down over there

İlaç alıyor musunuz?
ilach aluhyor musunuz
Are you taking any
medicines?

İlaç alerjiniz var mı?
ilach alerzhiniz varmuh
Are you allergic to any
medicines?

Tetanos aşınız var mı?
tetanos ashuhnuhz varmuh
Have you had a tetanus
injection?

Bugün ne yediniz?
bugewn ne yediniz
What have you eaten today?

**Barsaklarınız normal
çalışıyor mu?**
*barsaklaruhnuhz normal
chaluhshuhyormu*
Are your bowel movements
regular?

İltihap var
iltihap var
There's an infection

Gıda zehirlenmesi olmuş
guhda zehirlenmesi olmush
You have/He/she has food
poisoning

Bu bir kalp krizi
bu bir kalp krizi
This is a heart attack

İğne yapmam lazım
i:ne yapmam la:zuhm
I have to give an injection

Dikiş yapmam lazım
dikish yapmam la:zuhm
I'll have to stitch it up

Röntgen lazım
röntgen la:zuhm
An X-ray is necessary

Kan/İdrar tahlili lazım
kan/idrar tahlili la:zuhm
A blood/urine test is
necessary

Size bir reçete yazacağım
size bir rechete yazaja:uhm
I'll write you a prescription

**Günde üç defa bir tablet/
hap alın**
*gewnde ewch defa bir tablet/
hap aluhn*
Take one tablet three times
a day

Yemeklerden önce/sonra
yemeklerden önje/sonra
Before/After meals

Aç karnına
ach karnuhna
On an empty stomach

Yatarken
yatarken
At bedtime

Dinlenmeniz lazım
dinlenmeniz la:zuhm
You must rest

Üç gün yatak istirahati lazım
ewch gewn yatak istirahati la:zuhm
He/she/you must stay in bed for three days

Beş gün sonra tekrar gelin
besh gewn sonra tekrar gelin
Come back in five days' time

Bol su içmeniz lazım
bol su ichmeniz la:zuhm
You must drink plenty of water

Bol likid almanız lazım
bol likid almanuhz la:zuhm
You must drink plenty of liquids

Hiç bir şey yemeyeceksiniz
hich bir shey yemeyejeksiniz
You should eat nothing

Hastaneye yatmanız lazım
hasta:neye yatmanuhz la:zuhm
You must go into hospital

Önemli bir şey değil
önemli bir shey de:il
It's nothing serious

Bir şeyiniz yok
bir sheyiniz yok
There's nothing wrong with you

Giyinebilirsiniz
gi:yinebilirsiniz
You can get dressed

At the dentist's
You may want to say

I want to see the dentist
Dişçiyi görmek istiyorum
dishchiyi görmek istiyorum

I have a toothache
Dişim ağrıyor
dishim a:ruhyor

This tooth hurts
Bu diş ağrıyor
bu dish a:ruhyor

I've broken my tooth
Dişim kırıldı
dishim kuhruhlduh

I've lost a filling
Dolgum düştü
dolgum dewshtew

I've lost a crown
Kronum düştü
kronum dewshtew

He/she has toothache
Dişi ağrıyor
dishi a:ruhyor

He/she has broken his/her tooth
Dişi kırıldı
dishi kuhruhlduh

He/she has lost a filling
Dolgusu düştü
dolgusu dewshtew

He/she has lost a crown
Kronu düştü
kronu dewshtew

Could you fix it temporarily?
Geçici olarak takabilir misiniz?
gechiji olarak takabilir misiniz

Could you give an injection?
Bir iğne yapar mısınız?
bir i:ne yapar muhsuhnuhz

This denture is broken
Bu takma diş kırıldı
bu takma dish kuhruhlduh

Could you repair it?
Tamir edebilir misiniz?
ta:mir edebilir misiniz

How much will it cost?
Kaç para tutar?
kach para tutar

You may hear

Ağzınızı açın
a:zuhnuhzuh achuhn
Open your mouth

Dolgu yapmam lazım
dolgu yapmam la:zuhm
I have to do a filling

Dişi çekmem lazım
dishi chekmem la:zuhm
I have to extract it

Size bir iğne yapacağım
size bir i:ne yapaja:uhm
I'm going to give you an injection

Parts of the body

English	Turkish	Pronunciation
Ankle	**Ayak bileği**	*iyak bile:i*
Appendix	**Apandis**	*apandis*
Arm	**Kol**	*kol*
Artery	**Damar**	*damar*
Back	**Sırt**	*suhrt*
Bladder	**Mesane**	*mesa:ne*
Blood	**Kan**	*kan*
Body	**Vücut**	*vewjut*
Bone	**Kemik**	*kemik*
Bottom	**Alt**	*alt*
Bowels	**Bağırsak**	*ba:uhrsak*
Breast	**Meme**	*meme*
Buttock	**Kaba et**	*kaba et*
Cartilage	**Kıkırdak**	*kuhkuhrdak*
Chest	**Göğüs**	*gö:ews*
Chin	**Çene**	*chene*
Ear	**Kulak**	*kulak*
Elbow	**Dirsek**	*dirsek*
Eye	**Göz**	*göz*
Face	**Yüz**	*yewz*
Finger	**Parmak**	*parmak*
Foot	**Ayak**	*iyak*
Genitals	**Cinsel organlar**	*jinsel organlar*
Gland	**Bez**	*bez*
Hair	**Saç**	*sach*
Hand	**El**	*el*
Head	**Baş**	*bash*
Heart	**Kalp**	*kalp*
Heel	**Topuk**	*topuk*
Hip	**Kalça**	*kalcha*
Jaw	**Çene**	*chene*
Joint	**Eklem**	*eklem*
Kidney	**Böbrek**	*böbrek*

Knee	**Diz**	*diz*
Leg	**Bacak**	*bajak*
Ligament	**Lif**	*lif*
Lip	**Dudak**	*dudak*
Liver	**Karaciğer**	*karaji:er*
Lung	**Akciğer**	*akji:er*
Mouth	**Ağz**	*a:uhz*
Muscle	**Kas**	*kas*
Nail	**Tırnak**	*tuhrnak*
Neck	**Boyun**	*boyun*
Nerve	**Sinir**	*sinir*
Nose	**Burun**	*burun*
Penis	**Penis**	*penis*
Private parts	**Cinsel organlar**	*jinsel organlar*
Rectum	**Rektum**	*rektum*
Rib	**Kaburga**	*kaburga*
Shoulder	**Omuz**	*omuz*
Skin	**Deri**	*deri*
Spine	**Belkemiği**	*belkemi:i*
Stomach	**Mide**	*mi:de*
Tendon	**Tendon**	*tendon*
Testicles	**Testis**	*testis*
Thigh	**But**	*but*
Throat	**Gırtlak**	*guhrtlak*
Thumb	**Başparmak**	*bashparmak*
Toe	**Ayak parmağı**	*iyak parma:uh*
Tongue	**Dil**	*dil*
Tonsils	**Bademcik**	*bademjik*
Tooth	**Diş**	*dish*
Vagina	**Vajina**	*vazhina*
Vein	**Damar**	*damar*
Wrist	**Bilek**	*bilek*

PROBLEMS AND COMPLAINTS

(For car breakdowns, see page 38; see also Emergencies, page 284)

• The police force is in charge of security in urban areas. It has different sections dealing with such matters as traffic control etc. The police carry arms in Turkey.

• In rural areas, a military force called **jandarma** is responsible for law and order.

• If the service is not satisfactory in a hotel or restaurant and your complaints are ignored by the management, you can write directly to the Ministry of Tourism (**Turizm Bakanlığı** – address, page 188).

You may see

Emniyet Müdürlüğü	Police headquarters
Emniyet Teşkilatı	Police force
Jandarma	Military police force
Karakol	Police station
Polis	Police
Trafik Polisi	Traffic police

You may want to say

General phrases

Could you help me?
Bana yardım eder misiniz?
bana yarduhm edermisiniz

Could you fix it
(immediately)?
(Hemen) tamir eder misiniz?
(hemen) ta:mir eder misiniz

When can you fix it?
Ne zaman tamir edersiniz?
ne zaman ta:mir edersiniz

Can I speak to the manager?
Müdürle konuşabilir miyim?
*mewdewrle konushabilir
mi-yim*

There's a problem
Bir problem var
bir problem var

There isn't/aren't any ...
... yok
... yok

I need ...
Bana ... lazım
bana ... la:zuhm

I want ...
... istiyorum
... istiyorum

The ... doesn't/don't work
... çalışmıyor
... chaluhshmuhyor

The ... is/are broken
... kırık
... kuhruhk

The ... is/are out of order
... bozuk
... bozuk

It wasn't my fault
Benim suçum yok
benim suchum yok

I've forgotten ...
... unuttum
... unuttum

I've lost ...
... kaybettim
... kiybettim

We've lost ...
... kaybettik
... kiybettik

... has/have been stolen
... çalındı
... chaluhnduh

... has/have disappeared
... yok oldu
... yok oldu

... isn't/aren't here
... burada yok
... burada yok

The ... is/are missing
... kayıp
... kiyuhp

Something's missing
Bir şey kayıp
bir shey kiyuhp

This isn't mine
Bu benim değil
bu benim de:il

Where you're staying

There isn't any (hot) water
(Sıcak) su yok
(suhjak) su yok

There's no light
Işık yok
uhshuhk yok

There isn't any toilet paper
Tuvalet kağıdı yok
tuvalet ka:uhduh yok

The shower doesn't work
Duş çalışmıyor
dush chaluhshmuhyor

There isn't any electricity
Elektrik yok
elektrik yok

The lock's broken
Kilit kırık
kilit kuhruhk

There aren't any towels
Havlu yok
havlu yok

The switch on the lamp is broken
Lambanın düğmesi kırık
lambanuhn dew:mesi kuhruhk

I need another pillow
Bir yastık daha lazım
bir yastuhk daha la:zuhm

I can't open the window
Pencereyi açamıyorum
penjereyi achamuhyorum

I need another blanket
Bir battaniye daha lazım
bir battani-ye daha la:zuhm

I can't turn the tap off
Musluğu kapatamıyorum
muslu:u kapatamuhyorum

I need a light bulb
Ampul lazım
ampul la:zuhm

The toilet doesn't flush
Tuvalet çalışmıyor
tuvalet chaluhshmuhyor

The wash-basin is blocked
Musluk tıkanmış
musluk tuhkanmuhsh

It's too hot in the room
Oda çok sıcak
oda chok suhjak

The wash-basin is dirty
Musluk kirli
musluk kirli

The bed's very uncomfortable
Yatak çok rahatsız
yatak chok rahatsuhz

The room is too dark
Oda çok karanlık
oda chok karanluhk

There's a lot of noise
Çok gürültü var
chok gewrewltew var

The room's too small
Oda çok küçük
oda chok kewchewk

There's a smell of gas
Gaz kokuyor
gaz kokuyor

In bars and restaurants

This is undercooked
Bu az pişmiş
bu az pishmish

This is dirty
Bu kirli
bu kirli

This is burnt
Bu yanmış
bu yanmuhsh

This smells bad
Bu kötü kokuyor
bu kötew kokuyor

This is cold
Bu soğuk
bu so:uk

This tastes strange
Bunun tadı tuhaf
bunun taduh tuhaf

I didn't order this
Ben bunu istemedim
ben bunu istemedim

There's a mistake on the bill
Hesapta bir yanlışlık var
hesapta bir yanluhshluhk var

This glass is cracked
Bu bardak çatlak
bu bardak chatlak

In shops

I bought this here (yesterday)
Bunu (dün) buradan aldım
bunu (dewn) buradan alduhm

Could you change this for me?
Bunu değiştirir misiniz?
bunu de:ishtirir misiniz

I want to return this
Bunu geri vermek istiyorum
bunu geri vermek istiyorum

Could you refund me the money?
Parayı geri verir misiniz?
pariyuh geri verir misiniz

Here's the receipt
Makbuz burada
makbuz burada

It has a flaw
Defo var
defo var

It has a hole
Delik var
delik var

There's a stain/mark
Leke var
leke var

This is off/rotten
Bu bozulmuş
bu bozulmush

This isn't fresh
Bu taze değil
bu ta:ze de:il

There is no lid
Kapak yok
kapak yok

Forgetting and losing things and theft

I've forgotten my ticket
Biletimi unuttum
biletimi unuttum

I've forgotten the key
Anahtarı unuttum
anahtaruh unuttum

I've lost my wallet
Cüzdanımı kaybettim
jewzdanuhmuh kiybettim

I've lost my driving licence
Ehliyetimi kaybettim
ehli-yetimi kiybettim

We've lost our rucksacks
Sırt çantalarımızı kaybettik
*suhrt chantalaruhmuhzuh
kiybettik*

I've lost my rucksack
Sırt çantamı kaybettim
suhrt chantamuh kiybettim

Where's the lost property
office?
Kayıp eşya bürosu nerede?
kayuhp eshya bewrosu nerede

Where's the police station?
Karakol nerede?
karakol nerede

My bag's been stolen
Çantam çalındı
chantam chaluhnduh

My car's been stolen
Arabam çalındı
arabam chaluhnduh

My money's been stolen
Param çalındı
param chaluhnduh

My earrings are missing
Küpelerim kayıp
kewpelerim kiyuhp

If someone's bothering you

Leave me alone!
Beni rahat bırakın!
beni rahat buhrakuhn

Go away, or I'll call the
police
Git, yoksa polis çağırırım
git yoksa polis cha:ruhruhm

Someone's bothering me
Birisi beni rahatsız ediyor
birisi beni rahatsuhz ediyor

Someone's following me
Birisi beni takip ediyor
birisi beni ta:kip ediyor

You may hear

Helpful and unhelpful replies

Bir dakika lütfen
bir dakika lewtfen
Just a moment, please

Tabii
tabii
Of course

Buyurun
buyurun
Here you are

Hemen değiştireyim
hemen de:ishtireyim
I'll change it immediately

Yarın hazır olur
yaruhn hazuhr olur
It'll be ready by tomorrow

Maalesef mümkün değil
maalesef mewmkewn de:il
Unfortunately it's not
    possible

Özür dilerim, ama yapamam
özewr dilerim ama yapamam
I'm sorry, but I can't

Maalesef yapacak bir şey yok
maalesef yapajak bir shey yok
Unfortunately there is
    nothing that can be done

Ben sorumlu (kişi) değilim
ben sorumlu (kishi) de:ilim
I'm not (the person)
    responsible

Biz sorumlu değiliz
biz sorumlu de:iliz
We're not responsible

Polise haber verin
polise haber verin
Report it to the police

En iyisi ...
en iyisi ...
The best thing would be ...

Questions you may be asked

Ne zaman aldınız?
ne zaman alduhnuhz
When did you buy it/them?

Makbuz yanınızda mı?
makbuz yanuhnuhzdamuh
Have you got the receipt?

Ne zaman oldu?
ne zaman oldu
When did it happen?

Nerede kaybettiniz?
nerede kiybettiniz
Where did you lose it/them?

Nerede çalındı?
nerede chaluhnduh
Where was it/were they stolen?

Çantanız nasıldı?
chantanuhz nasuhlduh
What is your bag like?

Arabanız nasıldı?
arabanuhz nasuhlduh
What is your car like?

Ne marka?
ne marka
What make is it?

Arabanızın plakası kaç?
arabanuhzuhn plakasuh kach
What's the registration number of your car?

İsminiz ne?
isminiz ne
What's your name?

Soyadınız ne?
soyaduhnuhz ne
What is your surname?

Adresiniz ne?
adresiniz ne
What's your address?

Nerede kalıyorsunuz?
nerede kaluhyorsunuz
Where are you staying?

Oda numaranız kaç?
oda numaranuhz kach
What's your room number?

Kaç numaralı daire?
kach numaraluh daire
What's the number of the flat?

Pasaportunuzun numarası kaç?
pasaportunuzun numarasuh kach
What's your passport number?

Sigortanız var mı?
sigortanuhz varmuh
Are you insured?

Bu formu doldurun lütfen
bu formu doldurun lewtfen
Please fill in this form

154

BASIC GRAMMAR

How Turkish works

Turkish uses endings added to words to express things that in English are expressed with a different word or several separate words (pronouns, parts of verbs, prepositions and so on).

For example, the ending **-lik** changes an adjective into a noun:

iyi	good	**iyilik**	goodness
güzel	beautiful	**güzellik**	beauty

And there are endings for things like 'with' and 'without':

süt milk   **sütlü** with milk   **sütsüz** without milk

Words can be built up using more than one ending. For example, **plajdayım** means 'I am on the beach':

plaj (the) beach   **-da** on/at/in   **-yim** I am

Vowel harmony

Different endings can have slightly different forms because of a feature of Turkish called vowel harmony. This means that the vowels in the endings change depending on what the last vowel of the basic word is. For example, the ending for 'with' can be **-li**, **-lü**, **-lı** or **-lu**:

şekerli	with sugar	**sütlü**	with milk
kremalı	with cream	**limonlu**	with lemon

Turkish has eight vowels, four of them called front vowels, four of them back vowels:

front vowels **e i ö ü**
back vowels **a ı o u**

Vowel harmony means that if the last vowel of the basic word is a front vowel, then the endings added to it will also have front vowels:

otel	hotel	**oteller**	hotels
güzel	beautiful	**güzellik**	beauty
süt	milk	**sütlü**	with milk
şeker	sugar	**şekersiz**	without sugar

But if the last vowel of the basic vowel is a back vowel, then the endings will have back vowels:

oda	room	**odalar**	rooms
hasta	ill	**hastalık**	disease
limon	lemon	**limonlu**	with lemon
tuz	salt	**tuzsuz**	without salt

Some endings can have two basic forms:

	front	*back*
plural	**-ler**	**-lar**
on/at/in	**-de**	**-da**

Some endings can have four basic forms:

	front	*back*
my	**-im, -üm**	**-ım, -um**
with	**-li, -lü**	**-lı, -lu**

Where there are four basic forms of an ending, you can tell which to use by what the last vowel of the basic word is:

last vowel	*vowel in ending*
e, i	i
ö, ü	ü
a, ı	ı
o, u	u

For example:

el	hand	**elim** my hand	**iş**	job	**işim** my job
göz	eye	**gözüm** my eye	**gül**	rose	**gülüm** my rose
baş	head	**başım** my head	**varış**	arrival	**varışım** my arrival
kol	arm	**kolum** my arm	**kuş**	bird	**kuşum** my bird

Vowel harmony seems rather complicated at first, but, with practice, choosing the right vowel will become instinctive. And if you get it wrong, the chances are that you'll still be understood.

Nouns

There is no definite article ('the') in Turkish. The indefinite article ('a' or 'an') is the same as the word for 'one' – **bir** – so that, for example, **bir bilet** means 'a ticket' or 'one ticket'.

The plural of a noun is formed by adding the ending **-ler** or **-lar**:

müze	museum	**müzeler**	museums
çocuk	child	**çocuklar**	the children

However, if there is a number before the noun, then the noun keeps the singular form:

bilet ticket   **iki bilet** two tickets   **biletler** tickets

Endings

Below are some of the most common endings that are added to nouns and pronouns. See the section on Vowel harmony (page 155) for how to decide which form of the ending to use. If you can't work out the correct form, at least try to get roughly the right sound – for instance, an *uhm* sound to mean 'my', a *de* sound to mean 'on/in/at', and so on.

Where several endings are added, plural endings come first, possessives next, prepositions last. For possessive endings, see page 160.

In some cases, if the basic word ends in a vowel, an extra consonant is added between the word and the ending.

to/for: **-e, -a**
Add **y** if the basic word ends in a vowel:

to the hotel	**otele**	to the beach	**plaja**
to the corner	**köşeye**	to the room	**odaya**

by/using/with: **-le, -la**
Add **y** if basic word ends in a vowel:

by train	**trenle**	with a knife	**bıçakla**
by ship	**gemiyle**	with water	**suyla**

on/in/at: **-de, -da, -te, -ta**
If the basic word ends in **ç, f, h, k, p, s, ş** or **t**, you add **-te** or **-ta**; otherwise, add **-de** or **-da**:

in the hotel	**otelde**	on the beach	**plajda**
on the bus	**otobüste**	on the bed	**yatakta**

from: **-den, -dan, -ten, -tan**
As above, if the basic word ends in **ç, f, h, k, p, s, ş** or **t**, you add **-ten** or **-tan**; otherwise, add **-den** or **-dan**:

from the hotel	**otelden**	from the beach	**plajdan**
from the food	**yemekten**	from the street	**sokaktan**

with, containing: **-li, -lü, -lı, -lu**

with sugar	**şekerli**	with milk	**sütlü**
with ice cream	**dondurmalı**	with salt	**tuzlu**

without: **-siz, -süz, -sız, -suz**

without sugar	**şekersiz**	without milk	**sütsüz**
without ice cream	**dondurmasız**	without salt	**tuzsuz**

When two nouns come together, one of them describing or qualifying the other, the second noun takes the ending **-i, -ü, -ı, -u**, with an extra **s** if the basic word ends in a vowel:

the Marmara hotel	**Marmara oteli**
lentil soup	**mercimek çorbası**

(see also Possessives, page 160)

When an ending is added to a proper noun (a name), in writing there's an apostrophe before the ending:

to Ali	**Ali'ye**	in Ankara	**Ankara'da**

Subject pronouns

'You'
In English there is only one way of addressing people – using the word 'you'. In Turkish there are two ways – informal and formal. Most of the phrases in this book use the formal way.

Sen is the informal way, and is used with people you know well.

Siz is the formal way of saying 'you'. It is also the plural, formal and informal.

I	ben
you (*informal*)	sen
he/she/it	o
we	biz
you (*formal/plural*)	siz
they	onlar

Subject pronouns are often omitted in speech, because the verb endings make it clear who or what the subject is (see Verbs, page 164).

Object pronouns

me	beni
you (*informal*)	seni
him/her/it	onu
us	bizi
you (*formal/plural*)	sizi
them	onları

As with nouns, various endings can be added to pronouns to express things such as 'to me', 'for him', 'from us', 'my' and so on.

to/for: **-e, -a**

(NB: the 'me' and 'you' forms begin with **ban-** and **san-**)

to/for me	**bana**
to/for you	**sana**
to/for him/her/it	**ona**
to/for us	**bize**
to/for you	**size**
to/for them	**onlara**

from: **-den, -dan**

from me	**benden**
from you	**senden**
from him/her/it	**ondan**
from us	**bizden**
from you	**sizden**
from them	**onlardan**

with: **-le, -la**, added to 'mine', 'yours', etc. (see below)

with me	**benimle**
with you	**seninle**
with him/her/it	**onunla**
with us	**bizimle**
with you	**sizinle**
with them	**onlarla**

Possessives

To say 'my ...', 'his ...', 'our ...' etc. you add the appropriate ending to the noun. The choice of vowels in the ending depends on the vowel harmony rules (see page 155). The endings are:

my	**-im, -üm, -ım, -um**
your	**-in, -ün, -ın, -un**
his/her/its	**-i, -ü, -ı, -u**
our	**-imiz, -ümüz, -ımız, -umuz**
your	**-iniz, -ünüz, -ınız, -unuz**
their	**-leri, -ları**

e.g.:

my house	**evim**
my husband/wife	**eşim**
his/her friend	**arkadaşı**
your passport	**pasaportunuz**

However, if you are putting a possessive ending after a word that ends in a vowel,

1 you add an **s** before the 'his/hers/its' ending, e.g.

room	**oda**	his/her room	**odası**
skin	**deri**	its skin	**derisi**
box	**kutu**	its box	**kutusu**

2 you drop the initial vowel of the other possessive endings, e.g.

| my room | **odam** |
| our car | **arabamız** |

'Mine', 'yours', etc.

mine	**benim**
yours	**senin**
his/hers/its	**onun**
ours	**bizim**
yours	**sizin**
theirs	**onların**

The same words are used to emphasise that something is '*my ...*', '*your ...*', etc.:

| *my* friend | **benim arkadaşım** |
| it's *our* room | **bizim odamız** |

In English, possession is also shown by putting 's after the possessor, e.g. 'John's car', 'Susan's house', 'the cat's whiskers'. Sometimes the word 'of' is used instead of the 's, e.g. 'the branches of the tree', 'the boot of the car', etc. In Turkish this is shown by adding an ending to the possessor. The endings are: -in, -ün, -ın, -un, with an extra **n** before these endings if the basic word ends in a vowel. In addition, the second noun must have the ending **-i**, **-ü**, **-ı** or **-u** with an **s** put before it if the basic word ends in a vowel (see page 157). For example:

the beach of the hotel	**otelin plajı**
the door of the room	**odanın kapısı**
Ali's friend	**Ali'nin arkadaşı**
the mosques of Istanbul	**İstanbul'un camileri**

Adjectives

Adjectives always come before the noun:

cold beer	**soğuk bira**
cheap hotel	**ucuz otel**
my clean towel	**temiz havlum**

Comparatives (-er, more)

The word **daha** is put before the adjective, e.g:

daha güzel	more beautiful
daha iyi	better
Bugün hava daha sıcak	The weather is warmer today

For 'than', you add the ending **-den**, **-dan**, **-ten**, **-tan**, e.g.:

Bugün hava dünden daha sıcak	The weather is warmer today than yesterday
İstanbul Ankara'dan daha büyük	Istanbul is bigger than Ankara
Bu otel o otelden daha ucuz	This hotel is cheaper than that hotel

Superlatives (-est, most)

The word **en** is put before the adjective, e.g.:

en iyi	best
en pahalı	most expensive
en kolay	easiest
en rahat	most comfortable
Hangi oda en güneşli?	Which room is the sunniest?
Hangi otel en ucuz?	Which hotel is the cheapest?

Demonstratives (this, that)

Adjectives

this, these	**bu**
that, those	**şu/o**

Bu oda çok rahat	This room is very comfortable
O otelin adı ne?	What's the name of that hotel?

When they are used as adjectives, **bu/şu/o** don't take the plural ending; only the noun takes the plural ending, e.g.:

O adamlar kim?	Who are those men?
Bu koltuklar rahat	These chairs are comfortable

Pronouns

When the demonstratives are used as pronouns, meaning 'this (one)', 'these (ones)', 'those (ones)', the singular ones are the same as the above (**bu/şu/o**). The plurals are:

these (ones)	**bunlar**
those (ones)	**şunlar/onlar**

For example:

Bu ucuz	This (one) is cheap
Bunlar çok güzel	These are very nice
Onlar ne?	What are those?

Verbs

For the verbs 'to be' and 'to have', see below.

Verbs are listed in dictionaries in the infinitive form (the equivalent of the English 'to ...'). Turkish infinitives end in **-mek** or **-mak**, e.g.:

to go **gitmek** to work **çalışmak**

Turkish verbs have endings for (i) the tense (present, past, future, etc.) and (ii) the subject of the verb (I, you, he, she, etc.). To use the verb in a sentence, remove the **-mek/-mak** ending and then add the appropriate endings to what's left (the stem).

Present tense

For the present tense, the endings are:
(i) For the tense:
  -iyor, -üyor, -ıyor or **-uyor** (according to the rules of vowel harmony)
  or simply **-yor** after a verb ending in a vowel – if the verb stem ends in **e** or **a**, then these vowels are replaced by **i** and **ı** respectively
(ii) For the subject:

I	**-um**	we	**-uz**
you	**-sun**	you	**-sunuz**
he/she/it	*(none)*	they	**-lar**

For example, 'to work' is **çalışmak**:

stem	*tense ending*	*person ending*		
çalış-	-ıyor	-um	I work	**çalışıyorum**

'To want' is **istemek**; the stem is **iste-** but the **e** changes to **i**:

	tense	*person*		
stem	*ending*	*ending*		
isti-	**-yor**	**-um**	I want	**istiyorum**

Some sample verbs:

	'want'	*'go'*	*'stay'*
I	**istiyorum**	**gidiyorum**	**kalıyorum**
you	**istiyorsun**	**gidiyorsun**	**kalıyorsun**
he/she/it	**istiyor**	**gidiyor**	**kalıyor**
we	**istiyoruz**	**gidiyoruz**	**kalıyoruz**
you	**istiyorsunuz**	**gidiyorsunuz**	**kalıyorsunuz**
they	**istiyorlar**	**gidiyorlar**	**kalıyorlar**

Note: There are very few irregular verbs in Turkish. One is **gitmek**: its stem for the present tense is **gid-** (not **git-**).

Negatives
To make a verb negative in the present tense, you add **-mi**, **-mü**, **-mı** or **-mu** to the stem before the **-iyor/-yor** ending:

I am not working	**Çalışmıyorum**
I do not want to go	**Gitmek istemiyorum**
We are not staying in this hotel	**Bu otelde kalmıyoruz**

Questions
To turn a statement into a question in the present tense, you add **mu-** before the person ending; in writing, the two parts of the verb are separate, though they are spoken as one word:

Are you going to Bodrum?	**Bodrum'a gidiyor musunuz?**
Do you want wine?	**Şarap istiyor musunuz?**
Is the tap working?	**Musluk çalışıyor mu?**

Past tense

The past tense works in the same way, but using different endings. The endings are:

(i) For the tense:
   -di, -dü, -dı, -du (or **-ti, -tü, -tı, -tu** after the consonants **ç, f, h, k, p, s, ş** or **t**)

(ii) For the subject:

I	**-m**	we	**-k**
you	**-n**	you	**-niz, -nüz, -nız, -nuz**
he/she/it	*(none)*	they	**-ler, -lar**

For example:

I worked	**Çalıştım**
We went to Ankara	**Ankara'ya gittik**
Last year I stayed at that hotel	**Geçen yıl o otelde kaldım**

Negatives

For the negative, you add **-me** or **-ma** before all the other endings, e.g.:

I didn't work	**Çalışmadım**
We didn't go to Ankara	**Ankara'ya gitmedik**
I didn't like this hotel	**Bu oteli beğenmedim**

Questions

To turn statements into questions in the past tense, you add **mi, mü, mı** or **mu** at the end of the sentence, e.g.:

Did you go to Ankara?	**Ankara'ya gittiniz mi?**
Did you like this meal?	**Bu yemeği beğendiniz mi?**

Future tense

There are other sets of endings for the future tense, but you can also use the present tense for talking about the future, especially if you use words like **yarın** (tomorrow) or **gelecek hafta** (next week) to make it clear you're talking about events in the future:

I am going tomorrow   **Yarın gidiyorum**

'To be'

To say 'there is/are', see below.

The present tense of the verb 'to be' is formed by adding endings to a noun or adjective, as always following the rules of vowel harmony (see page 155). A **y** is added as indicated after a basic word ending in a vowel. The endings are:

I am	**-(y)im, -(y)üm, -(y)ım, -(y)um**
you are (*informal*)	**-sin, -sün, -sın, -sun**
he/she/it is	**[-dir, -dür, -dır, -dur]**
we are	**-(y)iz, -(y)üz, -(y)ız, -(y)uz**
you are (*formal/plural*)	**-siniz, -sünüz, -sınız, -sunuz**
they are	**[-dir(ler), -dür(ler), -dır(lar), -dur(lar)]**

Note: The **-dir** and **-dir(ler)** endings and their variations are generally not used in spoken Turkish.

Some examples:

teacher	**öğretmen**	I am a teacher	**Öğretmenim**
English	**İngiliz**	We are English	**İngiliziz**
tired	**yorgun**	You are tired	**Yorgunsunuz**
hot	**sıcak**	The weather is hot	**Hava sıcak**

Negatives
For the negative of 'to be', the noun or adjective is unchanged and the endings are added to the separate word **değil**:

I am not a teacher	**Öğretmen değilim**
We are not English	**İngiliz değiliz**
You are not tired	**Yorgun değilsiniz**
The weather is not hot	**Hava sıcak değil**

Questions

For questions using 'to be', the noun or adjective is unchanged and the endings are added to **mi-**, **mü-**, **mı-** or **mu-**; in writing the two words are separate but they are spoken as one word:

Are you a teacher?	**Öğretmen misiniz?**
Are you English?	**İngiliz misiniz?**
Is the weather hot?	**Hava sıcak mı?**

Past tense

For the past tense of 'to be', you use the same endings as for other verbs, added to the appropriate noun or adjective, e.g.:

| I was a teacher | **Öğretmendim** |
| You were tired | **Yorgundunuz** |

For the negative, these endings are added to the word **değil**:

| I was not well | **İyi değildim** |
| You were not tired | **Yorgun değildiniz** |

For questions, again the noun or adjective is unchanged, and the past tense endings are added to **miy-**, **müy-**, **mıy-** or **muy-**:

| Were you a teacher? | **Öğretmen miydiniz?** |
| Was the weather hot? | **Hava sıcak mıydı?** |

'To have'

For the verb 'to have', you add the possessive ending to the thing possessed (see Possessives, page 160), and follow it with the word **var** for 'has/have', or **yok** for 'has/have not', e.g.:

| daughter | **kız** | I have one daughter | **Bir kızım var** |
| money | **para** | We don't have any money | **Paramız yok** |

For questions, you add **mı** after **var**, and **mu** after **yok**:
Do you have a room vacant? **Boş odanız var mı?**
Don't you have any children? **Çocuklarınız yok mu?**

'There is/are'

The words **var** and **yok** also mean 'there is/are' and 'there is/are not':
There is too much salt **Çok tuz var**
There is no shower in the room **Odada duş yok**

Again, for questions you add **mı** after **var**, and **mu** after **yok**:
Is there a restaurant in the hotel? **Otelde lokanta var mı?**
Isn't there any hot water? **Sıcak su yok mu?**

Question words

The position of question words (what?, who?, why?, where?, how? etc.) can vary, depending on what is being emphasised, but in general:

Question words come before the verb:
what? **ne?** What do you want? **Ne istiyorsunuz?**
where? **nerede?** Where do you live? **Nerede oturuyorsunuz?**
how? **nasıl?** How do I get to the beach? **Plaja nasıl giderim?**

But in questions where the verb is 'to be', the question words **ne?**, **nerede?** and **nasıl?** come at the end of the question:
What is your name? **İsminiz ne?**
Where is the beach? **Plaj nerede?**
How is the weather? **Hava nasıl?**

DAYS, MONTHS, DATES

Days

Sunday	**Pazar**	*pazar*
Monday	**Pazartesi**	*pazartesi*
Tuesday	**Salı**	*saluh*
Wednesday	**Çarşamba**	*charshamba*
Thursday	**Perşembe**	*pershembe*
Friday	**Cuma**	*juma*
Saturday	**Cumartesi**	*jumartesi*

Months

January	**Ocak**	*ojak*
February	**Şubat**	*shubat*
March	**Mart**	*mart*
April	**Nisan**	*nisan*
May	**Mayıs**	*miyuhs*
June	**Haziran**	*haziran*
July	**Temmuz**	*temmuz*
August	**Ağustos**	*a:ustos*
September	**Eylül**	*eylewl*
October	**Ekim**	*ekim*
November	**Kasım**	*kasuhm*
December	**Aralık**	*araluhk*

Seasons

spring	**ilkbahar**	*ilkbahar*
summer	**yaz**	*yaz*
autumn	**sonbahar**	*sonbahar*
winter	**kış**	*kuhsh*

General phrases

day	**gün**	*gewn*
week	**hafta**	*hafta*
fortnight	**onbeş gün**	*onbesh gewn*
month	**ay**	*iy*
year	**yıl**	*yuhl*
season	**mevsim**	*mevsim*
today	**bugün**	*bugewn*
tomorrow	**yarın**	*yaruhn*
yesterday	**dün**	*dewn*
(in the) morning	**sabah**	*sabah*
(in the) afternoon	**öğleden sonra**	*ö:leden sonra*
(in the) evening	**akşam**	*aksham*
(at) night	**gece**	*geje*
this morning	**bu sabah**	*bu sabah*
this afternoon	**bu öğleden sonra**	*bu ö:leden sonra*
this evening	**bu akşam**	*bu aksham*
tonight	**bu gece**	*bu geje*
tomorrow morning	**yarın sabah**	*yaruhn sabah*
tomorrow afternoon	**yarın öğleden sonra**	*yaruhn ö:leden sonra*
tomorrow evening	**yarın akşam**	*yaruhn aksham*
yesterday morning	**dün sabah**	*dewn sabah*
yesterday afternoon	**dün öğleden sonra**	*dewn ö:leden sonra*
last night	**dün gece**	*dewn geje*
on Monday	**Pazartesi**	*pazartesi*
on Tuesdays	**Salıları**	*saluhlaruh*
every Wednesday	**her Çarşamba**	*her charshamba*
in October	**Ekim'de**	*ekimde*
in spring	**ilkbaharda**	*ilkbaharda*

at the beginning of March	**Mart başında**	*mart bashuhnda*
in the middle of June	**Haziran ortasında**	*haziran ortasuhnda*
at the end of May	**Mayıs sonunda**	*miyuhs sonunda*
in six months' time	**altı ay sonra**	*altuh iy sonra*
during the summer	**yazın**	*yazuhn*
during the winter	**kışın**	*kuhshuhn*
two years ago	**iki yıl önce**	*iki yuhl önje*
in the '90s	**doksanlarda**	*doksanlarda*

last ...	**geçen ...**	*gechen ...*
last Monday	**geçen Pazartesi**	*gechen pazartesi*
last week	**geçen hafta**	*gechen hafta*
last month	**geçen ay**	*gechen iy*
last year	**geçen yıl**	*geçen yuhl*

next ...	**gelecek ...**	*gelejek ...*
next Friday	**gelecek Cuma**	*gelejek juma*
next week	**gelecek hafta**	*gelejek hafta*
next month	**gelecek ay**	*gelejek iy*
next year	**gelecek yıl**	*gelejek yuhl*

172

What day is it today?	**Bugün ne?**
	bugewn ne
What is the date today?	**Bugün ayın kaçı?**
	bugewn iyuhn kachuh
When is your birthday?	**Doğum gününüz ne zaman?**
	do:um gewnewnewz ne zaman
It's (on) the first of January	**Bir Ocak'ta**
	bir ojakta
(on) Tuesday 8th May	**Sekiz Mayıs'ta**
	sekiz miyuhsta
1993	**bin dokuz yüz doksan üç**
	bin dokuz yewz doksan ewch
the 20th century	**yirminci yüzyıl**
	yirminji yewzyuhl

TIME

There is no a.m./p.m. distinction in Turkish when you're talking about the time. Usually it will be understood whether you are referring to morning, afternoon or evening. But just to make sure you can add the Turkish for these and say **sabah dokuzda** (at nine in the morning), **akşam yedide** (at seven in the evening), **gece on birde** (at eleven at night) and so on.

What time is it?	**Saat kaç?**	saat kach
It's one o'clock	**Saat bir**	saat bir
It's two o'clock	**Saat iki**	saat iki
It's three o'clock	**Saat üç**	saat ewch
It's twelve o'clock	**Saat on iki**	saat on iki

To say 'at ... o'clock', you add the ending meaning 'at' to the number, **-de, -da, -te,** or **-ta**:

(At) what time?	**Saat kaçta?**	saat kachta
At one o'clock	**Saat birde**	saat birde
At three o'clock	**Saat üçte**	saat ewchte
At six o'clock	**Saat altıda**	saat altuhda

For times *past* the hour, the numbers have endings added:

1	**biri**	biri	7	**yediyi**	yedi-yi
2	**ikiyi**	iki-yi	8	**sekizi**	sekizi
3	**üçü**	ewchew	9	**dokuzu**	dokuzu
4	**dördü**	dördew	10	**onu**	onu
5	**beşi**	beshi	11	**on biri**	on biri
6	**altıyı**	altuhyuh	12	**on ikiyi**	on iki-yi

| It's five past eight | **Saat sekizi beş geçiyor** | saat sekizi besh gechiyor |
| At five past eight | **Saat sekizi beş geçe** | saat sekizi besh geche |

It's a quarter past ...	**Saat ... çeyrek geçiyor**	*saat ... cheyrek gechiyor*
At a quarter past ...	**Saat ... çeyrek geçe**	*saat ... cheyrek geche*
It's half past ...	**Saat ... buçuk**	*saat ... buchuk*
At half past ...	**Saat ... buçukta**	*saat buchukta*

But note:

It's half past twelve	**Saat yarım**	*saat yaruhm*
At half past twelve	**Yarımda**	*yaruhmda*

For times *to* the hour, the numbers have other endings added:

1	**bire**	*bire*	7	**yediye**	*yedi-ye*
2	**ikiye**	*iki-ye*	8	**sekize**	*sekize*
3	**üçe**	*ewche*	9	**dokuza**	*dokuza*
4	**dörde**	*dörde*	10	**ona**	*ona*
5	**beşe**	*beshe*	11	**on bire**	*on bire*
6	**altıya**	*altuhya*	12	**on ikiye**	*on iki-ye*

It's a quarter to ...	**Saat ... çeyrek var**	*saat ... cheyrek var*
At a quarter to ...	**Saat ... çeyrek kala**	*saat ... cheyrek kala*
It's ten to ...	**Saat ... on var**	*saat ... on var*
At ten to ...	**Saat ... on kala**	*saat ... on kala*

(in the) morning	**sabah**	*sabah*
(in the) afternoon	**öğleden sonra**	*ö:leden sonra*
(in the) evening	**akşam**	*aksham*
(at) night	**gece**	*geje*
midday	**öğle**	*ö:le*
at midday	**öğleyin**	*ö:leyin*
midnight	**gece yarısı**	*geje yaruhsuh*
at midnight	**gece yarısında**	*geje yaruhsuhnda*

minute	**dakika**	*dakika*
hour	**saat**	*saat*
a quarter of an hour	**bir çeyrek saat**	*bir cheyrek saat*
three quarters of an hour	**üç çeyrek saat**	*ewch cheyrek saat*

half an hour	**yarım saat**	*yaruhm saat*
exactly ...	**tam ...**	*tam ...*
approximately ...	**yaklaşık ...**	*yaklashuhk ...*
nearly ...	**neredeyse ...**	*neredeyse ...*
soon	**yakında**	*yakuhnda*
early	**erken**	*erken*
late	**geç**	*gech*
on time	**zamanında**	*zamanuhnda*
half an hour ago	**yarım saat önce**	*yaruhm saat önje*
in ten minutes' time	**on dakikaya kadar**	*on dakikiya kadar*

24-hour clock

At airports and stations, and also on the radio and television, the 24-hour clock is used.

0900	**saat dokuz**	*saat dokuz*
1300	**saat on üç**	*saat on ewch*
1430	**saat on dört otuz**	*saat on dört otuz*
2055	**saat yirmi elli beş**	*saat yirmi elli besh*

COUNTRIES AND NATIONALITIES

The adjective to describe things is the same as that used for
nationality, but without the -li ending (if there is one), e.g.
Çinli Chinese (*person*)
Çin Chinese (*thing*)   **Çin ipeği** Chinese silk

Country/Continent		Nationality
Afghanistan	**Afganistan**	**Afgan**
Africa	**Afrika**	**Afrikalı**
Albania	**Arnavutluk**	**Arnavut**
Algeria	**Cezayir**	**Cezayirli**
Armenia	**Ermenistan**	**Ermeni**
Asia	**Asya**	**Asyalı**
Australia	**Avustralya**	**Avustralyalı**
Austria	**Avusturya**	**Avusturyalı**
Azerbaijan	**Azerbaycan**	**Azeri**
Belgium	**Belçika**	**Belçikalı**
Bosnia	**Bosna**	**Boşnak**
Brazil	**Brezilya**	**Brezilyalı**
Bulgaria	**Bulgaristan**	**Bulgar**
Canada	**Kanada**	**Kanadalı**
China	**Çin**	**Çinli**
Croatia	**Hırvatistan**	**Hırvat**
Cyprus	**Kıbrıs**	**Kıbrıslı**
Czechoslovakia	**Çekoslovakya**	**Çek**
Denmark	**Danimarka**	**Danimarkalı**
Egypt	**Mısır**	**Mısırlı**
England	**İngiltere**	**İngiliz**
Europe	**Avrupa**	**Avrupalı**
Finland	**Finlandiya**	**Finlandiyalı**

France	Fransa	Fransız
Georgia	Gürcistan	Gürcü
Germany	Almanya	Alman
Great Britain	Büyük Britanya	
Greece	Yunanistan	Yunanlı
Hungary	Macaristan	Macar
Iceland	İzlanda	İzlandalı
India	Hindistan	Hintli
Iran	İran	İranlı
Iraq	Irak	Iraklı
Ireland	İrlanda	İrlandalı
Israel	İsrail	İsrailli
Italy	İtalya	İtalyan
Kuwait	Kuveyt	Kuveytli
Japan	Japonya	Japon
Jordan	Ürdün	Ürdünlü
Lebanon	Lübnan	Lübnanlı
Libya	Libya	Libyalı
Malta	Malta	Maltalı
Montenegro	Karadağ	Karadağlı
Morocco	Fas	Faslı
Netherlands	Hollanda	Hollandalı
New Zealand	Yeni Zelanda	Yeni Zelandalı
North America	Kuzey Amerika	Kuzey Amerikalı
Northern Ireland	Kuzey İrlanda	Kuzey İrlandalı
Norway	Norveç	Norveçli
Pakistan	Pakistan	Pakistanlı
Poland	Polonya	Polonyalı
Portugal	Portekiz	Portekizli
Romania	Romanya	Romanyalı
Russia	Rusya	Rus

Saudi Arabia	**Suudi Arabistan**	**Suudi**
Scotland	**İskoçya**	**İskoçyalı**
		İskoç (*things*)
Serbia	**Sırbistan**	**Sırp**
South America	**Güney Amerika**	**Güney Amerikalı**
Spain	**İspanya**	**İspanyol**
Sweden	**İsveç**	**İsveçli**
Switzerland	**İsviçre**	**İsviçreli**
Syria	**Suriye**	**Suriyeli**
Tunisia	**Tunus**	**Tunuslu**
Turkey	**Türkiye**	**Türk**
Ukraine	**Ukrayna**	**Ukraynalı**
United Kingdom	**Birleşik Krallık**	
United States of America	**Amerika Birleşik Devletleri/Amerika**	**Amerikalı** **Amerikan** (*things*)
Wales	**Galler Bölgesi**	**Galli**
Yugoslavia	**Yugoslavya**	**Yugoslav**

GENERAL SIGNS AND NOTICES

Açık	Open
Araç çıkışı	Vehicles exiting
Araç girişi	Vehicles entering
Araç giremez	No entry for vehicles
Asansör	Lift
Asansör bozuk	Lift out of order
Askeri bölge	Military zone
Bayanlar	Ladies
Baylar	Gentlemen
Bekleme odası/salonu	Waiting room
Bilet gişesi	Ticket office
Boş	Vacant
Bozuk	Out of order
Çalışma saatleri	Office hours
Çekiniz	Pull
Çıkış	Exit
Çimlere basmayınız	Do not step on the grass
Çöp	Litter
Çöp dökmek yasaktır	Dumping litter is forbidden
Danışma	Information
Denize girmek yasaktır	Bathing is forbidden
Dikkat	Attention, Beware
Dolu	Full, Occupied
Dokunmayınız	Do not touch
Dur	Stop
Durmak yasaktır	No stopping
Düğmeye basınız	Press the button
Erkeklere	For men
Gecikme	Delay
Giriş	Entrance
Girişi kapatmayınız	Do not obstruct the entrance

Giriş katı	Ground floor
Gişe	Ticket office
Gürültü etmeyiniz	Do not make a noise
İçecek su	Drinking water
İçme suyu	Drinking water
İmdat freni	Emergency brake
İndirim	Reductions
İtiniz	Push
Kadınlara	For women
Kalkış	Departure
Kapalı	Closed
Kapıyı kapayınız	Close the door
Kapıyı vurunuz	Knock on the door
Kasa	Cash desk
Kat	Floor
Kiralık	For rent/hire
Köpeğe dikkat	Beware of the dog
Kuru temizleme	Dry cleaning
Kuru yerde saklayınız	Keep in a dry place
Meşgul	Engaged
Ölüm tehlikesi	Danger of death
Özel	Private
Özel indirim	Special reductions
Pansiyon	Boarding house
Pencereden sarkmayınız	Do not lean out of the window
Otel	Hotel
Restoran	Restaurant
Satılık	For sale
Serin yerde saklayınız	Keep in a cool place
Sıcak	Hot
Sigara içilmez	No smoking
Sigara içmek yasaktır	Smoking is forbidden
Soğuk	Cold
Son kullanım tarihi	Use by

Şoförle konuşmak yasaktır	Speaking to the driver is forbidden
Tehlike	Danger
Tehlikeli virajlar	Dangerous bends
Tek yön	One way
Türk malı	Made in Turkey
Ucuzluk	Sale
Uzun araç	Long vehicle
Varış	Arrival
Vezne	Cashier
Yangın merdiveni	Fire escape
Yangın tehlikesi	Danger of fire
Yasak bölge	No-go area
Yavaş	(Go) slow
Yerlere tükürmeyiniz	Do not spit on the floor
Zemin kat	Ground floor
Ziyaret saatleri	Visiting hours

CONVERSION TABLES
(approximate equivalents)

Linear measurements

centimetres **santimetre (sm/cm)**
metres **metre (m)**
kilometres **kilometre (km)**

10 cm = 4 inches	1 inch = 2.45 cm
50 cm = 19.6 inches	1 foot = 30 cm
1 metre = 39.37 inches	1 yard = 0.91 m
(just over 1 yard)	
110 metres = 100 yards	
1 km = 0.62 miles	1 mile = 1.61 km

To convert
km to miles: divide by 8 and multiply by 5
miles to km: divide by 5 and multiply by 8

Miles		Kilometres
0.6	1	1.6
1.2	2	3.2
1.9	3	4.8
2.5	4	6.4
3	5	8
6	10	16
12	20	32
19	30	48
25	40	64
31	50	80
62	100	161
68	110	177
75	120	193
81	130	209

Liquid measures

litre **litre (l)**

1 litre = 1.8 pints	1 pint = 0.57 litre
5 litres = 1.1 gallons	1 gallon = 4.55 litres

'A litre of water's a pint and three quarters'

Gallons		Litres
0.2	1	4.5
0.4	2	9
0.7	3	13.6
0.9	4	18
1.1	5	23
2.2	10	45.5

Weights

gram **gram (g)**
kilo **kilo/kilogram (kg)**

100 g = 3.5 oz	1 oz = 28 g
200 g = 7 oz	¼ lb = 113 g
½ kilo = 1.1 lb	½ lb = 225 g
1 kilo = 2.2 lb	1 lb = 450 g

Pounds		Kilos (Grams)
2.2	1	0.45 (450)
4.4	2	0.9 (900)
6.6	3	1.4 (1400)
8.8	4	1.8 (1800)
11	5	2.3 (2300)
22	10	4.5 (4500)

Area

hectare **hektar**
1 hectare = 2.5 acres   1 acre = 0.4 hectares

To convert
hectares to acres: divide by 2 and multiply by 5
acres to hectares: divide by 5 and multiply by 2

Hectares		Acres
0.4	1	2.5
2.0	5	12
4	10	25
10	50	124
40.5	100	247

Clothing and shoe sizes

Women's dresses and suits

UK	10	12	14	16	18	20	
Continent	36	38	40	42	44	46	

Men's suits and coats

UK	36	38	40	42	44	46	
Continent	46	48	50	52	54	56	

Men's shirts

UK	14	14½	15	15½	16	16½	17
Continent	36	37	38	39	41	42	43

Shoes

UK	3	4	5	6	7	7.5	8	9	10	11
Continent	35	36	37	38	39	40	41	42	43	44

Waist and chest measurements

inches	28	30	32	34	36	38	40	42	44	46	48	50
centimetres	71	76	80	87	91	97	102	107	112	117	122	127

Tyre pressures

lb/sq in	15	18	20	22	24	26	28	30	33	35
kg/sq cm	1.1	1.3	1.4	1.5	1.7	1.8	2.0	2.1	2.3	2.5

NATIONAL HOLIDAYS

Yılbaşı	New Year's Day	1 January
Çocuk Bayramı	Children's Day	23 April
Gençlik ve Spor Bayramı	Youth and Sports Day	19 May
Zafer Bayramı	Victory Day	30 August
Cumhuriyet Bayramı	Republic Day	29–30 October

There are also two important Muslim religious festivals. The dates of these change from year to year:

● **Şeker Bayramı (Id-ul-Fitr)** which comes at the end of Ramadan (the month of fasting in Islam) and lasts three days

● **Kurban Bayramı (Id-ul-Adha)** which comes approximately two months and ten days after the **Şeker Bayramı**

USEFUL ADDRESSES

In the UK and Ireland

Turkish Tourist Office
Egyptian House
170 Piccadilly
London W1V 0JL
Tel: 071–734 8681

Turkish Embassy
43 Belgrave Square
London SW1X 8PA
Tel: 071–235 5252

Turkish Consulate General
Rutland Lodge
Rutland Gardens
London SW7 1BX
Tel: 071–589 0360

Turkish British Chamber of Commerce and Industry
360 Oxford Street
London W1N 9HA
Tel: 071–499 4265

THY Turkish Airlines
11 Hanover Street
London W1R 9NF
Tel: 071–499 9247

Turkish Embassy
11 Clyde Road
Ballsbridge
Dublin 4
Ireland
Tel: 1–685240

In Turkey

British Embassy
Şehit Ersan Caddesi 46/A
Çankaya – Ankara
Tel: (90 4) 4274310

British Vice-Consulate
1442. Sokak, No 49
Alsancak – İzmir
Tel: (90 51) 635151

British Consulate-General
Meşrutiyet Caddesi, No 34
Tepebaşı – İstanbul
Tel: (90 1) 2447540

Türkiye Turing ve Otomobil Kurumu
Şişli Meydanı
İstanbul

Ministry of Tourism
Gazi Mustafa Kemal Bulvarı, 33
Demirtepe
Ankara
Tel: (90 4) 231 73 80

NUMBERS

0	**sıfır**	*suhfuhr*
1	**bir**	*bir*
2	**iki**	*iki*
3	**üç**	*ewch*
4	**dört**	*dört*
5	**beş**	*besh*
6	**altı**	*altuh*
7	**yedi**	*yedi*
8	**sekiz**	*sekiz*
9	**dokuz**	*dokuz*
10	**on**	*on*
11	**on bir**	*on bir*
12	**on iki**	*on iki*
13	**on üç**	*on ewch*
14	**on dört**	*on dört*
15	**on beş**	*on besh*
16	**on altı**	*on altuh*
17	**on yedi**	*on yedi*
18	**on sekiz**	*on sekiz*
19	**on dokuz**	*on dokuz*
20	**yirmi**	*yirmi*
21	**yirmi bir**	*yirmi bir*
22	**yirmi iki**	*yirmi iki*
23, etc.	**yirmi üç**	*yirmi ewch*
30	**otuz**	*otuz*
31	**otuz bir**	*otuz bir*
32	**otuz iki**	*otuz iki*
33, etc.	**otuz üç**	*otuz ewch*
40	**kırk**	*kuhrk*
50	**elli**	*elli*
60	**altmış**	*altmuhsh*

70	**yetmiş**	*yetmish*
80	**seksen**	*seksen*
90	**doksan**	*doksan*
100	**yüz**	*yewz*
101	**yüz bir**	*yewz bir*
102	**yüz iki**	*yewz iki*
103, etc.	**yüz üç**	*yewz ewch*
200	**iki yüz**	*iki yewz*
300	**üç yüz**	*ewch yewz*
400	**dört yüz**	*dört yewz*
500	**beş yüz**	*besh yewz*
600	**altı yüz**	*altuh yewz*
700	**yedi yüz**	*yedi yewz*
800	**sekiz yüz**	*sekiz yewz*
900	**dokuz yüz**	*dokuz yewz*
1,000	**bin**	*bin*
1,500	**bin beş yüz**	*bin besh yewz*
2,000, etc.	**iki bin**	*iki bin*
1,000,000	**bir milyon**	*bir milyon*
2,000,000	**iki milyon**	*iki milyon*

When a noun is used with a number, the noun stays in the singular form, e.g. **bir bilet** (one ticket), **iki bilet** (two tickets). ('The tickets' would be **biletler**.)

Years

1993	**bin dokuz yüz doksan üç**	*bin dokuz yewz doksan ewch*
1453	**bin dört yüz elli üç**	*bin dört yewz elli ewch*

DICTIONARY

In the Turkish alphabet ç, ğ, ş, ö and ü come after c, g, s, o and u respectively. The letter ı comes before i.

Verbs are given in the infinitive form with the -mek or -mak ending. See Basic grammar, page 155, for the other endings verbs and nouns take.

Turkish-English

Words for food and drink are given in the Menu reader, page 96. See also General signs and notices, page 179, and the 'You may see' lists in the individual sections.

A

abla elder sister
abone subscription, subscriber
acaba I wonder ...
acayip strange
acele haste, hurry
  acele etmek to hurry
acenta agency
acı bitter; hot (*spicy*)
acıkmak to be hungry
  acıktım I am hungry
acımak to feel pain; to be sorry for
acil urgent

acil servis emergency service
aç hungry
açacak bottle-opener
açık open
açıklama explanation
açlık hunger; famine
açmak to open
ad name
ada island
adam man
aday candidate
adet custom, habit
adi ordinary, common
adres address

affetmek to forgive, to pardon

affedersiniz I am sorry; excuse me

afiş poster

afiyet olsun enjoy your meal

afyon opium

ağ fishing net; web

ağabey/ağbi elder brother

ağaç tree

ağır heavy; slow

ağırlık weight

ağız mouth

ağlamak to cry

ağrı pain

ağrımak to ache, to hurt

Ağustos August

ahbap friend

ahçı cook

ahize receiver (*telephone*)

ahlak morals

ahlaksız immoral

ahmak fool, stupid

aile family

... ait belonging to ..., concerning

ak white

akarsu running water

akaryakıt fuel oil, liquid fuel

akciğer lung

Akdeniz the Mediterranean Sea

akıcı fluent

akıllı clever

akılsız stupid, silly

akıntı current (*water*)

akmak to flow

akraba relative, relation

akrep scorpion

akşam evening

akşamleyin in the evening

akşam yemeği dinner

aktarma change (*transport*)

aktarma yapmak to change (*trains, etc.*)

aktif active

aktör actor

al red

alacak credit, claim

alacaklı creditor

alafranga in the European style

alan open space

alarm alarm

alaturka in the Turkish style

alay mockery; regiment

albay colonel

alçak low

alçı plaster of Paris

aldanmak to be deceived

aldatmak to deceive

alerji allergy
alet tool, instrument
alev flame
alfabe alphabet
alın forehead
alışmak to get used to
alışveriş shopping
  alışverişe çıkmak to go
  shopping
alkış applause
alkışlamak to applaud
alkol alcohol
Allah God
Allahaısmarladık goodbye
almak to take, to get
alo hello (*on the phone*)
alt bottom, under
altı six
altın gold
altıncı sixth
altmış sixty
altüst upside down
alyans wedding ring
ama but
ambulans ambulance
amca uncle
ameliyat surgery
an moment
ana mother (*colloquial*)
Anadolu Anatolia
anahtar key
anarşi anarchy

anayol main road
ancak but, however; only,
  just
anı recollection, memoirs
anıt monument
ani sudden
anlam meaning
anlamak to understand
anlaşma agreement
anlaşmak to come to an
  agreement
anlatmak to explain
anne mother
anneanne maternal
  grandmother
anormal abnormal
anten aerial
antika antique
apartman block of flats
apartman dairesi flat
apse abscess
aptal silly, foolish
apteshane lavatory, toilet
ara interval
araba car; carriage (*horse-
  drawn*)
araç vehicle
Aralık December
aralık ajar
aramak to look for, search
arasında between, amongst
araştırma research

arı bee
arıza breakdown
arızalı broken down, not functioning
arka back, reverse side
arkadaş friend
armağan present
arpa barley
artı plus, +
artık any more; left over
artırmak to increase
arzu wish, desire
asker soldier
askı hanger
asmak to hang
aş cooked food
aşçı cook

aşağı down, lower
aşı vaccination
aşık lover
　aşık olmak to fall in love
aşk love
ateş fire, fever
at horse
atlamak to jump
atmak to throw
avukat lawyer
ay moon, month
ayak foot
ayakkabı shoe
ayçiçeği sunflower
ayırmak to separate, set apart

ayna mirror
aynı same
ayrı separate
az a little, few

B

baba father
babaanne paternal grandmother
bacak leg
bagaj luggage, baggage
badem almond
　badem ezmesi marzipan
bağ vineyard; tie, lace
bağlamak to tie
bağlantı connection
bağırmak to shout
bağırsak intestine
bahar spring
bahçe garden
bahşiş tip
bakan minister
bakkal grocer
baklava pastry dessert
bakmak to look, to look after
bal honey
balık fish
balkon balcony
bana to me
banka bank

banliyö suburb
  banliyö treni suburban rail line
bardak glass
barış peace
basamak step
basın the press, newspapers
banyo bathroom
basit simple
baş head
baş ağrısı headache
baş dönmesi giddiness
başka other, different
başkent capital city
başlamak to begin
batı west
batmak to sink
battaniye blanket
Bay Mr
Bayan Mrs/Miss
bayrak flag
bazen sometimes
bazı some
bebek baby, doll
bedava free
beden size
beğenmek to like
bekar single
beklemek to wait
bel waist; spade
belediye municipality

belediye başkanı mayor
belediye binası town hall
belge document
belki perhaps
belli obvious
ben I
benzemek to look like
benzer similar
benzin petrol
benzin istasyonu petrol station
beraber together
berber barber
beyaz white
beyaz zehir cocaine
bıçak knife
bırakmak to leave
bıyık moustache
bilet ticket
biletçi ticket collector
bilet gişesi ticket office, box office
bilezik bracelet
bilgi information
bilgisayar computer
bilim science
bilinmeyen numaralar directory enquiries
bilmek to know
bina building
binicilik horse riding
biniş kartı boarding pass

bir one; a, an
bira beer
biraz a little
birinci first
  birinci sınıf first class
birkaç several, a few
bisiklet bicycle
bisküvi biscuit
bitirmek to finish
  (something)
bitişik next to
bitki plant
bize to us
bizi us
bizim our
blucin jeans
bluz blouse
bodrum basement
boğaz throat; strait
bomba bomb
boru pipe
boş empty
boşanmış divorced
boya paint
boyamak to paint,
  decorate
bozuk out of order
bozuk para small change
böcek insect
bronzlaşmak to get tanned
broş brooch
broşür brochure

buçuk half
bugün today
bulaşık washing up
  bulaşık yıkamak to wash
  up
bulaşık makinesi dishwasher
bulmak to find
bulut cloud
bulutlu cloudy
bulvar boulevard
burun nose
but thigh
buz ice
buzdolabı fridge
büfe kiosk (*selling snacks*)
büro office
bütün all
büyük big, large
büyükelçilik embassy
büyütmek to enlarge

C

cadde road
cam glass
cami mosque
cankurtaran ambulance
canlı alive, lively
casus spy
caz jazz
ceket jacket

cenaze funeral
cep pocket
cereyan draught; electric
  current
ceviz walnut
ceza fine; punishment
cilt skin, complexion
cilt temizleyici skin
  cleanser
cin gin
Cuma Friday
Cumartesi Saturday
cüzdan wallet

Ç

çabuk quick
  çabuk olmak to hurry up
çadır tent
çağırmak to call (*shout*);
  to invite
çakı penknife
çakmak lighter
çalar saat alarm clock
çalı bush
çalışmak to work
çalmak to steal; to ring
çamaşır laundry
çamaşır makinesi washing
  machine
Çanakkale Boğazı
  Dardanelles

çanta bag
çarpmak to crash
çarşaf sheet
Çarşamba Wednesday
çarşı market, bazaar,
  shops
çatal fork
çatal bıçak cutlery
çay tea
çek cheque
çek defteri cheque book
çekiç hammer
çekmek to pull
çengelli iğne safety pin
çeşme fountain
çeyrek quarter
çıkış exit
çıkmak to come out
çıplak nude
çiçek flower
çift double; pair
çiftçi farmer
çiftlik farm
çiğ raw
çiklet chewing gum
çimen grass
çips crisps
çirkin ugly
çizme boots
çocuk child
çocuk arabası pram
çocuk bakıcısı child-
  minder

çocuk bezi nappies
çoğu most (of)
çok very; many, much
çorap socks, stocking
çöp litter; rubbish
çöp tenekesi dustbin
çünkü because
çürük rotten; bruise

D

dağ mountain
daha more
daha az less; than
dahil included
daire flat; office
dakika minute

dalga wave
dalmak to dive
dam roof
damat son-in-law
damla drop
danışma information
dans etmek to dance
dar narrow
dava trial
davet invitation
  davet etmek to invite
dayı uncle (*maternal*)
-de/-da/-te/-ta on; at; in
dede grandfather
defol! get out! go away!

değer value
değerli valuable
değil not
değiştirmek to change
deli mad
delik hole
delikanlı teenager (*male*)
demek to mean; to say
demir iron
demiryolu railway
demlik teapot
-den/-dan/-ten/-tan from; of
deneme experiment, trial
denemek to try out
deniz sea
deprem earthquake
dere stream, brook
dergi magazine
derhal immediately
deri leather
derin deep
dernek society
ders lesson
devam etmek to continue
deve camel
devlet state
dış external
dışarı out, outside
dışında except
dibinde at the bottom of
diğer other
dik steep

dikkat attention, care
dikkatli careful
dikkat etmek to be careful
dikmek to sew; to plant
dil language; tongue
dilek wish
dilemek to wish
dilim slice
din religion
dinlemek to listen
dinlenmek to rest
dip bottom
dirsek elbow
diş tooth
dişçi dentist
diyapozitif slide (*film*)
diz knee
doğa nature
doğal natural
doğmak to be born
doğru correct; straight
doğu east
doğum günü birthday
dokunmak to touch
doküman document
dolap cupboard
doldurmak to fill
dolgu filling
dolma stuffed
dolma kalem pen
dolmuş shared taxi
dolu full; engaged, busy

domates tomato
domuz pig
don frost; underpants
dondurma ice-cream
dondurulmuş frozen
donmuş frozen
dosdoğru straight ahead
dost friend
doymak to be full (*food*)
döndürmek to turn around
dönmek to come back, to
  return
döviz foreign currency
dövme tattoo
dövmek to beat
dudak lip
dudak boyası lipstick
dul widow/widower
duman smoke
durak stop
durgun still, calm
durmak to stop
durum situation
duş shower
duvar wall
duygu feeling
duymak to hear
düğme button; switch
düğün wedding
dükkan shop
dün yesterday
dünya world

düş dream
düşman enemy
düşmek to fall
düşünmek to dream
düşürmek to cause to fall; to drop
düz flat
düzenlemek to organise
düzine dozen

E

-e/-a/-ye/-ya to
eczane chemist
efendim sir/madam; I beg your pardon
Ege Aegean
eğer if; saddle
eğlenmek to have fun
Ekim October
ekmek bread
ekşi sour
ek supplementary
el hand
el bagajı hand luggage
el çantası handbag
el feneri torch
el freni handbrake
el sanatları crafts
elbise dress
elçilik embassy
eldiven glove

elektrik electricity
elektrik süpürgesi vacuum cleaner
elektrikli eşya electrical appliances
elişi hand-embroidered
ellemek to touch
elma apple
elmas diamond
emanet left luggage
emekli pensioner
emin safe; sure
eminim I am sure
emniyet kemeri seat belt
emoroit piles
en most
en az at least
enfeksiyon infection
enişte brother-in-law
erik plum
erkek male; gents (toilets)
erkek arkadaş boyfriend
erkek kardeş brother
erken early
esas main
eski old (things)
esnasında during
eş wife/husband
eşarp scarf
eşek donkey
eşek arısı wasp
eşofman tracksuit

eşya furniture
et meat
etek skirt
etiket label
ev house
evet yes
evli married
evrak documents
evrak çantası briefcase
Eylül September

F

fabrika factory
fakat but
fakir poor
far headlight; eye shadow
fare mouse
fark difference
fasulye beans
fatura invoice
fazla too much, excessive
fazla bagaj excess baggage
felaket disaster
fener lighthouse; torch, lamp
feribot car ferry
fermuar zip
fındık hazelnut
fırça brush
fırın bakery; oven
fırtına storm

fikir idea
film film
fincan cup
fiş plug; receipt
fiyat price
flaş flash
flört etmek to flirt
fotoğraf photo
fotoğraf çekmek to photograph
fotoğrafçı photographer
fotoğraf makinesi camera
fön blow-dry
fren brake
fren yapmak to brake

G

Galler Wales
garip strange
garson waiter
gazete newspaper
gazete bayii newsagent
gazino restaurant with show; open-air café
gazlı fizzy, with gas
gebe pregnant
gece night
gece kulübü nightclub
gecelik nightdress
gece yarısı midnight
gecikme delay

geç late
  geç kalmak to be late
geçen last, past
geçerli valid
geçit crossing, pass
geçmek to pass; to overtake
gelecek future; next
gelenek custom, tradition
geleneksel traditional
Gelibolu Gallipoli
gelin daughter-in-law
gelişmek to develop
  gelişmekte olan ülkeler developing countries
gelmek to come
gemi ship
genç young
genel general
genellikle generally
geniş wide
gerçek truth; genuine
gerçekten really
gerekli necessary
geri back, behind; backward
getirmek to bring
gıda foodstuff, nourishment
  gıda zehirlenmesi food poisoning
gibi like

gidiş single (*ticket*)
gidiş dönüş return (*ticket*)
giriş entrance
girmek to enter
gitmek to go
giyim eşyası clothing
giyinmek to get dressed
giymek to put on
gizli secret
göğüs chest; breast
gök sky
gök gürültüsü thunder
gök kuşağı rainbow
göl lake
gölge shadow
gölgede in the shade
gömlek shirt
göndermek to send
görmek to see
görümce sister-in-law
gösteri show; demonstration
göstermek to show
göz eye
gözlük spectacles
gözlükçü optician
gri grey
grip flu
grup group
güçlü strong
gül rose
güle güle goodbye

gülmek to laugh
gülünç ridiculous
gümrük customs
gümrüksüz duty free
gümüş silver
gün day
günaydın good morning
günce dairy
güneş sun
güneş banyosu sunbathing
güneşli sunny
güney south
gürültü noise
gürültülü noisy
güverte deck
güzel beautiful, nice

H

haber news
hafif light
hafta week
hafta sonu weekend
hala aunt (*paternal*)
halat rope
halı carpet
Haliç Golden Horn
halk people
hamam Turkish bath
hamamböceği cockroach
hangi which
hanım lady

hap pill
hapishane prison
hapşırmak to sneeze
harabe ruin
harcamak to spend
hardal mustard
hareket etmek to move
hariç except; external
harita map
hasta ill; patient
hastabakıcı nurse
hastalık disease
hastane hospital
hata mistake
hatıra souvenir; memoirs
hatırlamak to remember
hatta even
hava air; weather
havaalanı airport
havalimanı airport
hava tahmini weather forecast
havayolu airline
havlu towel
havuç carrot
havuz pond
hayat life
hayır no
hayvan animal
hayvanat bahçesi zoo
hazımsızlık indigestion
hazır ready

hazırlamak to prepare
hazırlık preparation
Haziran June
hediye present (gift)
hela lavatory
hemen immediately
  hemen hemen almost
hemşire nurse
hemzemin geçit level
  crossing
henüz just; yet
hep all; always
hepimiz all of us
hepsi all of it/them
her each; every
herkes everyone
herşey everything
her zaman always
hesap bill
hesap makinesi calculator
heyecan excitement
hıçkırık hiccups
Hıristiyan Christian
hırka cardigan
hırsız thief
hırsızlık theft
hız speed
hızlı fast
hiç (bir şey) nothing
hiç kimse nobody
hijyenik bağ sanitary towel
hikaye story

hindi turkey
his feeling
hisar fortress
hissetmek to feel
hizmet service
  hizmet etmek to serve
hizmetçi servant
horlamak to snore
hostes stewardess
hoş fine; nice
hoş geldiniz welcome
hoşlanmak to like
hükümet government
hürriyet freedom

I

ılık warm
ırza geçmek to rape
ısırmak to bite
ısıtma heating
ıslak wet
ısmarlamak to order
ıspanak spinach
ışık light
ızgara grilled

İ

iade etmek to give back
iç inside
  iç çamaşırı underwear

içeri inside
için for
içki drink (*alcoholic*)
içme suyu drinking water
içmek to drink
iğne needle
  iğne olmak to have an injection
iğrenç disgusting
ikamet residence
iki two
ikinci second
iklim climate
ilaç medicine
ile with, by
ileri forward
ileride further on; in future
iletmek to forward
ilgi attention, care
ilginç interesting
ilişki contact
ilk first
ilkbahar spring
ilk yardım first aid
imdat! help!
imza signature
imzalamak to sign
inanmak to believe
ince thin
İncil New Testament
incitmek to hurt

indirim reduction
indirimli satış sale
inek cow
inmek to get off
insan man, mankind
ip string
ipek silk
iplik thread
iptal etmek to cancel
iri large, big
İsa Jesus
ishal diarrhoea
iskele pier, landing area; scaffolding
iskemle chair
İslam Islam
İslami Islamic
İstanbul Boğazı Bosphorus
istasyon station
istemek to want; to request
iş job; business; work
işitme cihazı hearing aid
işitmek to hear
işlek busy
işsiz unemployed
iştah appetite
itfaiye fire brigade
itmek to push
iyi good, well
iyimser optimistic
izin permission; leave
izin vermek to allow

J

jambon ham
jilet razor blade
jandarma military police force
jelatin gelatine
jest gesture
jeton metal token
jöle jelly

K

kaba rude
kabız constipation
kabin memuru steward
kabuk shell
kabul etmek to accept
kaburga rib
kaç how many, how much
kaçak leak
kaçırmak to miss (*train etc.*); to abduct
kadar as
kadın woman
kağıt paper
  kağıt mendil tissues
kahvaltı breakfast
kahve coffee
kahverengi brown
kakao cocoa; hot chocolate

kalabalık crowd; crowded
kaldırım pavement
kale castle
kalem pencil
kalın thick
kalite quality
kalkış departure
kalkmak to take off; to get up
kalmak to stay
kalorifer central heating
kalp heart
kalp krizi heart attack
kamara cabin
kamyon lorry
kamyonet van
kan blood
kan grubu blood type
kanamak to bleed
kanun law
kapak lid
kapalı closed
kapamak to close; to switch off
kapatmak to close
kapı door
kaplıca spa
kaptan captain
kar snow
kara black
Karadeniz Black Sea
karanlık dark

karar decision
  karar vermek to decide
karınca ant
karışık mixed
karıştırmak to mix
karides prawn
karşı against; opposite
karşılamak to meet
karşılaşmak to come across
kart card
kartpostal postcard
kartvizit visiting card
kasa cash desk; strongbox
kasap butcher, butcher's
kase bowl
kaset cassette
Kasım November
kaş eyebrow
kaşık spoon
kaşıntı itch
kat floor
kavga fight
kavşak junction
kaya rock
kayak skiing
kaybetmek to lose
kaybolmak to get lost; to disappear
kaygan slippery
kayık rowing boat
kayınbirader brother-in-law

kayınpeder father-in-law
kayıp lost
kayıp eşya lost property
kayıt register, registration
kaymak thick cream
kaymak to slide; to skid
kaynana mother-in-law
kaynamış boiled
kaynar su boiling water
kaz goose
kaza accident
kazak jersey, sweater
kazanmak to win; to earn
keçi goat
kedi cat
kek cake
kel bald
kelebek butterfly
kelime word
kemer belt
kemik bone
kenar edge
kendi him/her/itself; own
kepenk shutters
kere time(s)
kerpeten pliers
kesik cut, cut off
kesmek to cut
kestane chestnut
kestirme shortcut
kılçık fishbone
kır countryside

kırık broken
kırmak to break
kırmızı red
kırtasiyeci stationer's
kısa short
kıskanç jealous
kış winter
kıyı coast
kıyma mince
kız girl
kızarkadaş girlfriend
kızartmak to fry
kızıl red
kibrit match
kilim flat-weave rug
kilise church
kilit lock
kilitlemek to lock
kim who
kime to whom
kimin whose
kimlik identity
   kimlik kartı identity card
kira rent
kiralamak to rent
kiralık for hire; to let
kirli dirty; polluted
kişi person(s)
Kitab-ı Mukaddes Bible
kitap book
kitapçı bookstore
klima air-conditioning

klimalı air-conditioned
koca husband; huge
koklamak to sniff
kokmak to give off a smell
koku smell; perfume
kol arm; handle
kol saati watch
kolay easy
koli package
kolye necklace
kompartıman compartment
komşu neighbour
konser concert
konserve tinned food
konsolosluk consulate
kontak lens contact lens
kontrol etmek to check
konuk guest
konuşmak to speak, to
   talk
-den/-dan/-ten/-tan korkmak
   to be afraid of
korku fear
korkunç horrible
korumak to protect
koşmak to run
kova bucket
koymak to put
koyun sheep
köpek dog
köprü bridge
kör blind

köşe corner
kötü bad
köy village
kral king
kraliçe queen
kravat tie
krem cream (*cosmetic*)
krem şantiye whipped cream
krema cream
kuaför hairdresser
kulak ear
kule tower
kullanışlı practical
kullanmak to use
kulüp club
kum sand
kumaş fabric
kurşun kalem pencil
kuru dry
  kuru temizleyici dry-cleaner
kurum society; organisation
kurumak to (become) dry
kurutmak to (make something) dry
kuş bird
kuşet couchette
kutu box
kuyruk tail; queue
kuyumcu jeweller's

kuzen cousin
kuzey north
kuzu lamb
küçük small
külot underpants
külotlu çorap tights
kül ash
kül tablası ashtray
küpe earring
Kuran Koran, Qur'an
kütüphane library; bookcase

L

lamba lamp
lastik rubber; tyre
lavabo basin
lazım necessary, needed
-le/-la with, by
leke stain
lezzetli delicious
-li/-lü/-lı/-lu with; containing
likör liqueur
liman port; harbour
limon lemon
lisan language
lokanta restaurant
lokum Turkish delight
Londra London
lütfen please

M

maç match (*sports*)
maden suyu mineral water
mağara cave
makarna pasta
makas scissors
makbuz receipt
makyaj make-up
makyaj malzemesi cosmetics
mal property
manav greengrocer
Manş Denizi English
  Channel
mantar mushroom; cork
manto women's coat
manzara scenery
Mart March
martı seagull
masa table
masa örtüsü table-cloth
masa tenisi table tennis
matbu printed matter
mavi blue
Mayıs May
mayo swimsuit
mazot diesel
mektup letter
-meli, -malı must; have to
meme breast
memnun glad
  memnun oldum I am
  pleased; pleased to meet
  you

memur official; civil
  servant
mendil handkerchief
merak hobby
merdiven ladder; stairs
merhaba hello
merhem ointment
mesaj message
mesela for example
meslek profession
meşgul engaged
mevsim season
meydan square
meyve fruit
mezarlık cemetery
minare minaret
misafir guest
mobilya furniture
moda fashion
mola pause; rest
mor purple
motosiklet motorcycle
mum candle
musluk tap; wash-basin
mutfak kitchen
mutlu happy
mücevher jewel
mücevherat jewellery
mümkün possible
mürettebat crew
müsaade etmek to allow
müshil laxative

Müslüman Muslim
müthiş terrific
müze museum
müzik music

N

nahoş unpleasant
nakit cash
namaz moslem prayer
nargile hookah,
 waterpipe
nasıl how
nazik polite; kind
ne what
 ne haber? how are
  things?
 ne kadar? how much?
 ne zaman? when?
ne ... ne neither ... nor
neden why
nedeniyle because of
nefes breath
 nefes almak to breathe
nefis delicious; excellent
nehir river
nem moisture
nemlendirici krem
 moisturiser
nerede where
niçin why
Nisan April

nişanlanmak to get
 engaged
nişanlı engaged
Noel Christmas
numara number

O

o he/she/it; that
Ocak January
ocak cooker
oda room
oda hizmetçisi chambermaid
oğlan boy
oğul son
okul school
okumak to read
olağan usual
olay event
oldukça quite
olgun ripe
olmak to be; to become;
 to happen
ona to him/her/it
onu him/her/it
orada there
orası there; that place
ordu army
orman forest
orta middle; medium
Osmanlı Ottoman
ot grass

otobüs bus
  otobüs durağı bus-stop
otomobil car
otopark car park
otostop hitchhike
otoyol motorway
oturacak yer seat
oturmak sit down; reside
oturma odası living room
oynamak to play (*games*)
oyun play; game
oyuncak toy

Ö

öbür gün the day after
  tomorrow
ödemek to pay
ödemeli reverse charge
  call
ödünç borrowed
  ödünç almak to borrow
  ödünç vermek to lend
öğle midday
  öğleden sonra in the
    afternoon
  öğle yemeği lunch
  öğleyin at midday
öğrenci student
öğrenmek to learn
öğretmek to teach
öğretmen teacher

öksürmek to cough
öksürük cough
ölçek scale
ölçmek to measure
ölçü measurement
öldürmek to kill
ölmek to die
ölü dead
ölüm death
ön front
önce before; ago
önem importance
önemli important
önemsiz unimportant
öneri suggestion
önermek to suggest; to
  advise
öpmek to kiss
öpücük kiss
ördek duck
örgü knitting
örmek to knit
örnek example
örneğin for example
örümcek spider
öyle such; so
öyleyse in that case; then
özel private
  özel ulak special
    delivery
özellikle especially
özlemek to miss

özür apology
  özür dilemek to apologise
  özür dilerim I am sorry
özürlü disabled

P

pahalı expensive
paket parcel
paketlemek to wrap up
palto overcoat
pamuk cotton
pansiyon guest house
pantolon trousers
para money
parça piece; part
pardon excuse me
park park
  park etmek to park
parmak finger
parmaklık fence; railings
Paskalya Easter
pasta cake, gateau
pastane café; cake shop
patates potato
patlak burst; punctured
patlamak to explode; to burst; to get punctured
patlıcan aubergine
patron boss
pay share

paylaşmak to share
Pazar Sunday
pazar market
Pazartesi Monday
peçete napkin
pek very
pek az very little
pek değil not much
pembe pink
pencere window
perde curtain
perhiz diet
peron platform
Perşembe Thursday
peşin in advance
peynir cheese
pikap record player
pil battery
pipo pipe
pire flea
pirinç rice (*uncooked*); brass
pişirmek to cook
pişmiş cooked
plaj beach
plak record
plaka number plate
plan plan; map
polis police
politika politics
pop müziği pop music
porsiyon portion

portakal orange
portatif portable
posta post
postacı postman
postalamak to post
postane post office
prens prince
prenses princess
prezervatif condom
priz socket
program programme
protesto protest
  protesto etmek to protest
protez dentures
PTT Post Office
pul stamp
puro cigar

puset push-chair
pusula compass

R

radyatör radiator
raf shelf
rahat comfortable
rahatsız uncomfortable; unwell
rahatsız etmek to bother; to pester
rahip priest
rakip rival
randevu appointment

ranza bunk bed
rastlamak to come across
razı agreeing, in agreement
  razı olmak to accept; to agree
reçel jam
reçete prescription
rehber guide
renk colour
renkli in colour; colourful
resepsiyon reception
resim picture
resmi official
  resmi tatil public holiday
rezervasyon reservation
rıhtım quay
rimel mascara
roman novel
rota route
römork trailer
röntgen X-ray
ruj lipstick
rüya dream
rüzgar wind

S

saat hour; clock, watch
  saat kaç? what time is it?
sabah morning
sabun soap

saç hair
saç kurutma makinesi hairdrier
sadece only
saf pure
sağ right; alive
sağanak downpour
sağır deaf
sağlığınıza! your health!
sağlık health
sağlıklı healthy
sağol thanks
sahil shore; coast
sahip owner
  sahip olmak to possess
sahte false; imitation
sakal beard
sakin calm; quiet
sakinleşmek to calm down
sakinleştirici tranquilliser
saklamak to hide; to keep
salata salad
saldırgan aggressive; aggressor
saldırı attack
Salı Tuesday
salyangoz snail
saman nezlesi hay fever
sana to you
sanat art
sanat galerisi art gallery
sanatçı artist

sanayi industry
saniye second
sara epilepsy
saralı epileptic
saray palace
sargı bandage
sarhoş drunk
  sarhoş olmak to get drunk
sarı yellow
sarışın blond
sarmak to wrap
sarmısak garlic
satılık for sale
satın almak to buy
satış sale
satmak to sell
savaş war, battle
sayfa page
saz Turkish string instrument; reed
sebze vegetable
seçmek to choose
sel flood
selam! hail!, greetings!
semaver samovar
sempatik appealing (*person*)
semt district
sen you
seni you
sepet basket
serbest free

sergi exhibition
serin cool
sert hard
servis service
  servis (ücreti) dahildir
    service (charge) is
    included
servis istasyonu garage
ses voice
sessiz silent
sessizlik silence
sevgi love
sevişmek to make love
sevmek to love
seyahat travel
seyahat acentası travel
  agent's
seyahat çeki traveller's
  cheque
seyirci audience, spectator
seyretmek to watch
sıcak hot
sıcaklık heat; temperature
sıfır zero
sığ shallow
sık frequent
  sık sık often
sıkı tight
sıkıcı boring
sıkışmak to get stuck
sınıf class
sınır border; limit

sıra row
sırasında during
sırt back
sırt çantası backpack
sızı dull pain
sızıntı leak
sızmak to leak
sigara cigarette
  sigara içilmez no
    smoking
  sigara içmek to smoke
sigorta fuse; insurance
silah weapon
silgi eraser
silmek to erase; to wipe
sinek fly
sinema cinema
sinir nerve
sinirli nervous
sinyal signal
sipariş order
sirke vinegar
sis fog
sivilce pimple
sivrisinek mosquito
siyah black
  siyah beyaz black and
    white
siz you
-siz/-süz/-sız/-suz without
size to you
sizi you

soğan onion
soğuk cold
soğuk algınlığı cold
  (*ailment*)
sokak street
sokmak to sting; to insert
sol left
solak left-handed
son end
sonbahar autumn
sonra then; afterwards
  -den/-dan sonra after ...
  bugünden sonra after
  today
sonradan later
sormak to ask (*question*)
soru question
sorumlu responsible
sorun problem
soyadı surname
soymak to peel; to undress
soyunmak to get undressed
söndürmek to blow out,
  put out (*fire, etc.*)
sönmek to be blown out
sönük dull; lacklustre
sörf surf
  sörf yapmak to surf
söylemek to say
söz words; promise
  söz vermek to promise
sözlü oral; betrothed

spiral IUD
spor sports
su water
suni artificial
sur city walls
susamak to be thirsty
  susadım I'm thirsty
... suyu ... juice
süet suede
sünger sponge
sünnet circumcision
süpürge broom
süper super
sürahi jug
süre period
sürgü bolt; bedpan
sürmek to drive
sürpriz surprise
sürü herd; flock
sürücü driver
sürücü belgesi driving
  licence
süt milk
sütlü with milk
sütsüz without milk
sütun column, pillar
sütyen bra

Ş

şahane wonderful
şair poet

şaka joke
şal shawl
şamandıra buoy
şampuan shampoo
şans luck
  iyi şanslar! good luck!
şapka hat
şarap wine
şarkı song
  şarkı söylemek to sing
şaşırmak to be surprised
şato castle
şehir city; town
  şehir merkezi city
  centre
şeker sugar
şeker hastalığı diabetes
  şeker hastası diabetic
şemsiye umbrella
şerefe! cheers!
şey thing
şezlong deck chair
şikayet complaint
  şikayet etmek to
  complain
şilte mattress
şimdi now
şirket company
şiş swelling; skewer
şişe bottle
şişman fat
şoför chauffeur

şoför ehliyeti driving
  licence
şok shock
şort shorts
şöyle böyle so-so
şu that
Şubat February
şunlar those

T

tabak plate
tabanca shotgun
tabii of course
tabldot set menu
tahta wood
takım team; set
takip etmek to follow
takmak to put on (*glasses,
  jewellery*)
takvim calendar
talebe student
talep demand
talih luck
talk pudrası talcum powder
tamam OK; all right
tamamlamak to complete
tamir repair
  tamir etmek to repair
tam whole
  tam pansiyon full board
  tam zamanında on time

tanık witness

tanımak to recognise; to know a person

tanışmak to be introduced

tanıştırmak to introduce

tanıtmak to introduce

Tanrı God

tansiyon blood pressure

tarak comb

taramak to comb

tarife timetable; recipe

tarih date; history

tarla field

tas bowl

taş stone

taşımak to carry

taşıt vehicle

taşmak to overflow

tat flavour

tatil holiday

tatlı sweet; dessert

tatmak to taste

tava fried; frying pan

tavan ceiling

tavla backgammon

tavsiye recommendation

  tavsiye etmek to recommend

tavşan rabbit

tavuk chicken

taze fresh

tazminat conpensation

tebrik congratulation

  tebrik etmek to congratulate

tehlike danger

tehlikeli dangerous

tek single, one

tek kişilik single (*bed, room, etc.*)

Tekel bayii kind of off-licence

tekerlek wheel

tekerlekli sandalye wheelchair

teklif etmek to propose

tekrar again

tekrarlamak to repeat

tel wire

teleferik cable-car

telefon telephone

  telefon etmek to ring, to phone

  telefon kodu dialling code

telgraf telegram

tembel lazy

temiz clean

temizlemek to clean

temizleyici cleansing

temizlikçi cleaner

Temmuz July

temsilci representative

tencere saucepan

tenzilat reduction
tepe hill
tepsi tray
tercüme translation
  tercüme etmek to translate
tercih preference
  tercih etmek to prefer
ter sweat
terlemek to sweat
terlik slipper
terzi tailor
tesisatçı plumber
teşekkür etmek to thank
  teşekkür ederim thank you
  teşekkürler thanks
teyp tape
teyze aunt (*maternal*)
tıkaç plug
tıkamak to block
tıkalı blocked
tıraş shave
tıraş fırçası shaving brush
tıraş olmak to shave
tırnak nail
tırnak cilası nail varnish
tirbuşon corkscrew
tişört T-shirt
tiyatro theatre
tok not hungry
top ball

toplantı meeting
toplu iğne pin
toprak earth
topuk heel
tornavida screwdriver
torun grandchild
tost toasted sandwich
toz dust
tören ceremony
trafik traffic
Trakya Thrace
tren train
tuğla brick
turuncu orange colour
tutmak to hold; to rent
tutuklamak to arrest
tutuşmak to fire
tutuşturmak to set fire to
tuvalet toilet, lavatory
tuvalet kağıdı toilet paper
tuz salt
tuzlu salty; salted
tükenmez ballpoint pen
tüm all
tümüyle altogether
tünel tunnel
tüpgaz Calorgas
Türk kahvesi Turkish coffee
tütün tobacco

U

ucuz cheap
uçak aeroplane
uçak seferi flight
uçmak to fly
uçurum precipice
uçuş flight
ufak small
ufuk horizon
ulus nation
uluslararası international
ummak to hope
umut hope
un flour
unutmak to forget
usta master workman
utangaç shy
utanmak to be shy
uyandırmak to awaken
uyanık awake
uyanmak to wake up
uyku sleep
  uykum geldi I'm sleepy
uyku ilacı sleeping pill
uyku tulumu sleeping bag
uyruk nationality
uyumak to sleep
uyuşturucu drugs
uzak far
uzaklık distance
uzanmak to lie down

uzman expert
uzun long
uzun boylu tall
uzunluk length
uzuv organ, limb

Ü

ücret fee; salary, wage
üç three
ülke country
ünlü famous
üst top
üst baş clothes, attire
üstünde on top of
ütü iron
ütülemek to iron
üvey anne stepmother
üvey baba stepfather
üzgün sad
üzülmek to regret
üzüm grapes
üzüntü worry; sadness

V

vaaz sermon
vadi valley
vagon carriage
vagon restoran dining car
vajina vagina
vali governor

valiz suitcase
vana valve
vantilatör fan
vapur steam-boat
var there is/are
varış arrival
varmak to arrive
vatan native country
vazo vase
ve and
vejeteryen vegetarian
vergi tax
vermek to give
vestiyer cloakroom
veteriner vet
veya or
vezne cash desk (*bank*)
vida screw
video video
viraj bend (*road*)
viski whisky
vitamin vitamins
vize visa
vurmak to hit
vücut body

Y

ya ... ya either ... or
yabancı foreign; foreigner
yabani wild
yağ fat; oil

yağlı greasy
yağmak to rain
yağmur rain
  yağmur yağıyor it is
  raining
yağmurluk raincoat
Yahudi Jewish
yaka collar
yakalamak to catch
yakın near
yakında nearby; soon
yakışıklı handsome
yakıt deposu fuel tank
yaklaşık approximately
yakmak to burn
yalan lie
  yalan söylemek to lie
yalı waterside residence
yalnız alone; only
yan side
yangın fire
yangın söndürme cihazı fire
  extinguisher
yanık burn
yanıt answer
yanıtlamak to answer
yankesici pickpocket
yanlış wrong; mistake
yanmak to get burnt
yapı building
yapma artificial
yapmak to make, to do

yaprak leaf
yar cliff
yara wound
yaralamak to injure
yaralanmak to get injured
yaralı injured
yararlı useful
yardım help
  yardım etmek to help
yarım half
  yarım pansiyon half board
yarın tomorrow
yasa law
yasak forbidden, prohibited
yastık pillow
yaş age; damp
  kaç yaşındasınız? how old are you?
yaşam life
yaşamak to live
yaşlı old
yat yacht
yatak bed
yatak odası bedroom
yatak takımı bed-linen
yataklı vagon sleeping-car
yatışmak to calm down
yatmak to go to bed
yavaş slow
  yavaş yavaş slowly

yay spring; bow
yaya pedestrian
yaya geçidi pedestrian crossing
yayan on foot
yaz summer
yazık! what a pity!
yazı makinesi typewriter
yazmak to write
yedek spare, extra
yedek parça spare parts
yeğen nephew
yelken sails
yelkenli sailing boat
yemek meal; dish; to eat
  yemek yediniz mi? have you eaten?
yemek listesi menu
yemek salonu dining room
yemek tarifi recipe
yenge sister-in-law (*brother's wife*)
yengeç crab
yeni new
  Yeni Yıl New Year
  Yeni yılınız kutlu olsun Happy New Year
yepyeni brand new
yer seat; place; ground
  yer ayırtmak to make a reservation
yer fıstığı peanut

yeşil green
yeter enough
yetişkin adult
yıkamak to wash
  something
yıkanmak to get washed
yıl year
yılan snake
Yılbaşı New Year's Eve
yıldız star
yıldönümü anniversary
yiyecek foodstuffs
yok there isn't/aren't
yoksa otherwise
yol path, way
yolcu passenger
  yolcu otobüsü coach
yolculuk journey
yorgan quilt
yorgun tired
yön direction
yönetici manager
yukarı up; upstairs
yumurta egg
yumurtalık eggcup
yumuşak soft
yurt homeland; residential
  hall for students
  yurt dışı abroad;
  overseas
yutmak to swallow
yuvarlak round

yüksek high
  yüksek sesle in a loud
  voice
yün wool
yürümek to walk
yürüyüş walk
yürüyüşe çıkmak to go for
  a walk
yüz face; a hundred
yüzde per cent
yüzme swimming
  yüzmeye gitmek to go
  swimming
yüzme havuzu swimming
  pool
yüzmek to swim
yüzük ring
yüzyıl century

Z

zaman time
  ne zaman when
  o zaman then; in that
  case
zamk glue
zarar damage; loss
  zarar vermek to damage
zarf envelope
zarif elegant
zavallı! poor thing!
zayıf thin; weak

zehir poison
zeki intelligent; clever
zemin kat basement
zengin rich
zeytin olive
zeytinyağı olive oil

zil bell
zincir chain
ziyaret visit
  ziyaret etmek to visit
zor difficult
zührevi hastalık VD

ENGLISH–TURKISH

There's a list of car parts on page 41, and parts of the body on page 145. See also the lists on pages 170–178.

A

a/an **bir**
about (*on the subject of*)
  hakkında
  (*approximately*)
  yaklaşık
above (*upstairs etc.*)
  yukarıda
  (*on top of*) **üstünde**
abroad **yurtdışı**
  to go abroad **yurt**
  dışına gitmek
abscess **apse**
to accept **kabul etmek**
accident **kaza**
accommodation
  kalacak yer
according to ... ... **göre**
account (*bank*) **hesap**
accountant **hesap**
  uzmanı
ache **ağrı**
acid **asit**
across **karşı**
acrylic **akrilik**

activity **faaliyet**
actor **aktör**
actress **aktris**
adaptor **adaptör**
address **adres**
adhesive tape **seloteyp**
admission **giriş**
adult **büyük**
advance: in advance
  peşin
advanced (*level*) **ileri**
advertisement **reklam**
to advertise **ilan etmek**
aerial **anten**
aeroplane **uçak**
afford: I can't afford it
  param yetmez
afraid: to be afraid
  korkmak
after **sonra**
afterwards **sonra**
afternoon **öğleden sonra**
aftershave **traş losyonu**
again **tekrar**
against **karşı**

age **yaş**
agency **acenta**
ago **önce**
to agree **kabul etmek**
AIDS **AIDS**
air **hava**
  by air **uçakla**
air conditioning
  havalandırma, klima
air force **hava kuvvetleri**
airline **hava yolları**
air mattress **şişirme
  yatak**
airport **havaalanı**
aisle (*plane*) **yol**
alarm **alarm**
alarm clock **çalar saat**
alcohol **alkol**
alcoholic **alkollü**
alive **canlı**
all **hepsi**
allergic to **alerjik**
to allow **izin vermek**
all right (*agreed*) **tamam**
almond **badem**
alone **yalnız**
along **boyunca**
already **zaten**
also **hem de**
although **rağmen**
always **her zaman**
am: I am (*see page 167*)

ambition **hırs**
ambulance **ambülans**
among **arasında**
amount **miktar**
amusement park
  eğlence parkı
anaesthetic **uyuşturucu**
and **ve**
angry **kızgın**
  to be angry **kızmak**
animal **hayvan**
anniversary **yıldönümü**
anorak **anorak**
another **bir başka**
to answer **cevap vermek**
answer **cevap**
antibiotic **antibiyotik**
antifreeze **antifriz**
antique **antika**
antiseptic **antiseptik**
any **hiç**
anyone **kimse**
anything (*something*)
  bir şey
  anything else? **başka
  bir şey?**
anyway **her neyse**
anywhere **nerede olursa**
apart from **ayrı**
apartment **daire**
aperitif **aperitif**
appendicitis **apandisit**

apple **elma**
appointment **randevu**
approximately **yaklaşık**
apricot **kayısı**
arch **kemer**
archaeology **arkeoloji**
architect **mimar**
architecture **mimari**
are: you/we/they are (*see page 167*)
area (*surface*) **alan**
  (*region*) **bölge**
argument **tartışma**
arm **kol**
around **etrafında**
around the corner **köşeyi dönünce**
around here **buralarda**
to arrange (*organize*) **düzenlemek**
arrest: under arrest **tutuklu**
to arrest **tutuklamak**
arrival **varış**
to arrive **varmak**
art **sanat**
  art gallery **sanat galerisi**
  fine arts **güzel sanatlar**
arthritis **artrit**
artichoke **enginar**

article (*newspaper*) **makale**
artificial **yapay**
artist **sanatçı**
as (*like*) **gibi**
ash **kül**
ashtray **sigara tablası**
to ask (*question*) **sormak**
  (*request*) **istemek**
asparagus **kuşkonmaz**
aspirin **aspirin**
assistant **yardımcı**
  (*shop*) **tezgahtar**
asthma **astım**
at **-de/-da/-te/-ta** (*see page 158*)
athletics **atletizm**
atmosphere **hava**
to attack **saldırmak**
attractive **çekici**
aubergine **patlıcan**
auction **açık artırma**
aunt (*mother's sister*) **teyze**
  (*father's sister*) **hala**
  (*uncle's wife*) **yenge**
author **yazar**
automatic **otomatik**
autumn **sonbahar**
to avoid **kaçınmak**
away (*distance*) **uzakta**
awful **berbat**

B

baby **bebek**
baby food **mama**
baby's bottle **biberon**
babysitter **çocuk bakıcısı**
back (*rear*) **arka**
  at the back **arkada**
  (*body*) **sırt**
backward **geri**
backwards **geriye**
bad **kötü**
bag **çanta**
baggage **bagaj**
baker **fırıncı**
baker's **fırın**
balcony **balkon**
bald **kel**
ball (*football, tennis etc.*) **top**
ballet **bale**
ballpoint pen **tükenmez kalem**
banana **muz**
band (*music*) **orkestra**
bandage **bant**
bank **banka**
barber **berber**
basement **bodrum**
basket **sepet**
basketball **basketbol**

bath **banyo**
  to have a bath **banyo yapmak**
bathing costume **mayo**
bathroom **banyo**
battery (*torch, radio etc.*) **pil**
  (*car*) **akü**
bay **koy**
bazaar **çarşı**
to be **olmak** (*see also page 167*)
beach **plaj**
bean **fasulye**
beard **sakal**
beautiful **güzel**
because **çünkü**
bed **yatak**
bedroom **yatak odası**
bee **arı**
beef **dana**
beer **bira**
beetroot **pancar**
before **önce**
to begin **başlamak**
beginning **başlangıç**
behind **arka**
beige **bej**
to believe **inanmak**
  I believe so **sanıyorum**
bell (*church*) **çan**
  (*door*) **zil**

to belong to **ait olmak**
(*to be a member of*)
üye olmak
below **alt**
(*beneath*) **altında**
belt **kemer**
bend **viraj**
bent **kıvrık**
berth **kuşet**
beside (*next to*) **yanında**
besides **yanısıra**
best **en iyi**
better **daha iyi**
between **arasında**
beyond **ötesinde**
bib (*baby's*) **önlük**
Bible **Kitab-ı Mukaddes**
bicycle **bisiklet**
big **büyük**
bigger **daha büyük**
biggest **en büyük**
bill **hesap**
bin (*rubbish*) **çöp tenekesi**
binoculars **dürbün**
biology **biyoloji**
bird **kuş**
birthday **doğum günü**
biscuit **bisküvi**
bishop **piskopos**
a bit **biraz**
to bite **ısırmak**

bitter **acı**
black **siyah, kara**
black and white (*film*) **siyah beyaz**
black coffee **sütsüz kahve**
blanket **battaniye**
bleach **çamaşır suyu**
to bleed **kanamak**
blind **kör**
blind (*Venetian*) **jaluzi**
blister: to have a blister **su toplamak**
blocked (*pipe*) **tıkanmış** (*passage*) **kapalı**
blond **sarışın**
blood **kan**
blouse **bluz**
to blow (*wind*) **esmek**
blow-dry **fön**
blue **mavi**
boarding **biniş**
boarding card **biniş kartı**
boat **vapur**
by boat **vapurla**
body **vücut**
boiled (*liquid*) **kaynamış** (*food*) **haşlanmış**
boiled egg **rafadan yumurta**
hard-boiled egg **katı yumurta**

boiler **termosifon**
boiling **kaynar**
bomb **bomba**
bone **kemik**
  (*fish*) **kılçık**
book **kitap**
to book **ayırmak**
booking **rezervasyon**
booking office **bilet
  gişesi**
bookshop **kitapçı**
boot **çizme**
  (*car*) **bagaj**
border (*edge*) **kenar**
  (*frontier*) **hudut**
boring **sıkıcı**
both **ikisi**
bottle **şişe**
bottle-opener **açacak**
bottom **alt**
bow (*ship*) **burun**
  (*knot*) **fiyonk**
bow-tie **papyon kravat**
bowl **kase**
box **kutu**
box office **bilet gişesi**
boy **oğlan**
boyfriend **erkek
  arkadaş**
bra **sutyen**
bracelet **bilezik**
brain **beyin**

branch **dal**
  (*bank etc.*) **şube**
brand **marka**
brandy **kanyak**
brass **pirinç**
brave **cesur**
bread **ekmek**
to break **kırmak**
  I've broken **kırdım**
breakdown truck
  kurtarıcı
breakfast **kahvaltı**
to breathe **nefes almak**
brick **tuğla**
bricklayer **duvarcı**
bride **gelin**
bridegroom **damat**
bridge **köprü**
briefcase **evrak çantası**
to bring **getirmek**
  can you bring me ...?
  ... getirir misiniz?
British **İngiliz**
broad **geniş**
broad bean **bakla**
brochure **broşür**
broken **kırık**
bronchitis **bronşit**
bronze **bronz**
brooch **iğne**
broom **süpürge**

brother **erkek kardeş**
brother-in-law
    kayınbirader
brown **kahverengi**
bruise **morluk**
brush **fırça**
bucket **kova**
buffet car **yemekli**
    vagon
to build **inşa etmek**
building **bina**
bulb (*light*) **ampül**
bumper **çamurluk**
burn **yanık**
to burn **yanmak**
burnt **yanmış**
bus **otobüs**
    bus station **otogar**
    bus stop **durak**
    by bus **otobüsle**
bush **çalı**
business **iş**
    business trip **iş gezisi**
    businessman **iş adamı**
    businesswoman **iş**
        kadını
busy **meşgul**
but **ama**
butane gas **bütan gazı**
butcher's **kasap**
butter **tereyağı**
butterfly **kelebek**

button **düğme**
to buy **almak**
by **ile; -le/-la/-yle/-yla**
    (*see page 158*)

C

cabbage **lahana**
cabin **kabin**
café **pastane**
cake **kek**
cake shop **pastane**
calculator **hesap**
    makinesi
to call **çağırmak**
    (*phone*) **telefon etmek**
    I am called ... **ismim ...**
    he/she/it is called ...
        ismi ...
    what are you called?
        isminiz ne?
calm **sakin**
camera **fotoğraf**
    makinesi
camomile tea **papatya**
    çayı
to camp **kamp yapmak**
camping **kamping**
campsite **kamping yeri**
can (*tin*) **kutu**
canned **konserve**
can opener **konserve**
    açacağı

carafe **sürahi**
caravan **treyler**
caravan site **kamping yeri**
cardigan **hırka**
care (*attention*) **dikkat**
to take care of ... ... **bakmak**
careful **dikkatli**
careless **dikkatsiz**
carpenter **marangoz**
carpet **halı**
carriage (*railway*) **vagon**
carrier bag **naylon torba**
carrot **havuç**
to carry **taşımak**
to carry on **devam etmek**
cash: to pay cash **nakit para vermek**
to cash a cheque **çek bozdurmak**
cash desk (*in shops*) **kasa;** (*in banks*) **vezne**
cassette **kaset**
cassette player **teyp makinesi**
cat **kedi**
catalogue **katalog**
to catch (*train, bus etc.*) **yetişmek**
Catholic **katolik**
cauliflower **karnıbahar**

to cause **sebep olmak**
cave **mağara**
ceiling **tavan**
celery **kereviz**
cellar **bodrum**
cemetry **mezarlık**
centimetre **santimetre**
central **merkezi**
central heating **kalorifer**
centre **merkez**
century **yüzyıl**
certain **kesin**
certainly **kesinlikle**
certificate **sertifika**
chain **zincir**
chair **iskemle**
champagne **şampanya**
change (*money*) **bozuk para**
to change (*money*) **bozdurmak**
(*clothes*) **değiştirmek**
changing room **soyunma odası**
channel: English Channel **Manş Denizi**
charcoal **mangal kömürü**
charter flight **tarifesiz uçuş**
cheap **ucuz**
check (*pattern*) **kareli**

to check **kontrol etmek**
to check in **çek-in yapmak**
cheek **yanak**
cheers! **şerefe!**
cheese **peynir**
chef **ahçı**
chemist's **eczane**
chemist **eczacı**
chemistry **kimya**
cheque **çek**
cherry **kiraz**
chess **satranç**
chestnut **kestane**
chewing gum **çiklet**
chicken **tavuk**
chickenpox **suçiçeği**
child **çocuk**
children **çocuklar**
chimney **baca**
china **porselen**
chips **patates tava**
chocolate **çikolata**
to choose **seçmek**
chop **pirzola**
Christian **Hıristiyan**
Christmas **Noel**
church **kilise**
cigar **puro**
cigarette **sigara**
cigarette lighter **çakmak**
cinema **sinema**
cinnamon **tarçın**

circle **daire**
  (*theatre*) **balkon**
circus **sirk**
city **şehir**
civil servant **memur**
class **sınıf**
classical music **klasik müzik**
clean **temiz**
cleansing cream **temizleyici krem**
clear **açık**
clerk **katip**
clever **akıllı**
climate **iklim**
to climb **tırmanmak**
climber **dağcı**
clinic **poliklinik**
cloakroom **vestiyer**
clock **saat**
close by **yakın**
to close **kapamak**
closed **kapalı**
cloth (*for cleaning*) **bez**
clothes **elbiseler**
clothes peg **mandal**
cloud **bulut**
cloudy **bulutlu**
club **kulüp**
coach **otobüs**
coal **kömür**
coarse **kaba**

coast **kıyı**
coat **palto**
coat-hanger **askı**
cocktail **kokteyl**
coffee (*Turkish*) **kahve**
  (*instant*) **neskahve**
coin **madeni para**
cold **soğuk**
  I'm cold **üşüyorum**
  to have a cold **nezle**
    olmak
  I have a cold **nezle**
    oldum
  it's cold (*weather*)
    hava soğuk
collar (*shirt, jacket etc.*)
    yaka
  (*dog's*) **tasma**
colleague **iş arkadaşı**
to collect **toplamak**
  collection **kolleksiyon**
college **kolej**
colour **renk**
in colour **renkli**
  colour-blind **renk körü**
  comb **tarak**
to come **gelmek**
to come back **geri dönmek**
to come down **aşağı inmek**
  comedy **komedi**
to come in **girmek**
  come in! **girin!**

to come out **çıkmak**
comfortable **rahat**
comic (*magazine*) **çizgi**
  roman
commercial **ticari**
common (*shared*) **ortak**
communism **komünizm**
communist **komünist**
compact disk **kompakt**
  disk
company **şirket**
compared with **göre**
compartment
  kompartman
compass **pusula**
to complain **şikayet etmek**
complaint **şikayet**
completely **tamamen**
complicated **karışık**
composer **besteci**
compulsory **zorunlu**
computer **bilgisayar**
computer science
  bilgisayar bilimi
concert **konser**
concert hall **konser**
  salonu
condition **durum**
conditioner (*hair*)
  yumuşatıcı
condom **prezervatif**
conference **konferans**

to confirm **doğrulamak**
connection (*travel*)
 aktarma
conscious **kendinde**
conservation **koruma**
conservative
 muhafazakar
constipation **kabız**
consulate **konsolosluk**
to contact **temas etmek**
 I want to contact ...
 **... ile temas kurmak
 istiyorum**
contact lens **kontak
 lenz**
contact lens cleaner
 **kontak lenz
 temizleyicisi**
continent **kıta**
contraceptive
 prezervatif
contraceptive pill
 doğum kontrol hapı
contract **kontrat**
convenient **uygun**
 it's (not) convenient
 for me **benim için
 uygun (değil)**
cook **ahçı**
to cook **pişirmek**
cooker **ocak**
cool **serin**

copper **bakır**
copy **kopya**
cork **mantar**
corkscrew **tirbuşon**
corner **köşe**
correct **doğru**
corridor **koridor**
cosmetics **makyaj
 malzemesi**
cost **fiyat**
cot **bebek yatağı**
cotton (*thread*) **iplik**
 (*material*) **pamuklu**
cotton wool **pamuk**
couchette **kuşet**
cough **öksürük**
cough medicine **öksürük
 şurubu**
to count **saymak**
counter (*shop*) **tezgah**
country **ülke**
couple **çift**
course (*of lessons*) **kurs**
court (*law*) **mahkeme**
 (*tennis etc.*) **kort**
cousin **kuzen**
cover **örtü**
cover charge **servis
 ücreti**
cow **inek**
cramp **kramp**
crash (*car*) **kaza**

cream (*food*) **krema**
(*lotion*) **krem**
credit card **kredi kartı**
crescent **ay**
crisps **çips**
cross **haç**
to cross **geçmek**
crossroads **kavşak**
crowded **kalabalık**
crown (*tooth*) **kron**
cruise **deniz yolculuğu**
crutch **koltuk değneği**
to cry **ağlamak**
crystal **kristal**
cucumber **salatalık**
cufflinks **kol düğmesi**
cup **fincan**
cupboard **dolap**
cure **tedavi**
to cure **tedavi etmek**
curly **kıvırcık**
current (*electric*) **akım**
(*sea*) **akıntı**
curtain **perde**
cushion **yastık**
customs **gümrük**
cut **kesik**
to cut **kesmek**
cutlery **çatal bıçak**
cycling **bisiklete binmek**
cyclist **bisikletçi**
cystitis **sistit**

D

daily **günlük**
damaged **hasarlı**
damp (*living space*)
rutubetli
(*clothes, etc.*) **yaş**
dance **dans**
to dance **dans etmek**
danger **tehlike**
dangerous **tehlikeli**
dark **karanlık**
dark (*hair/skin*) **esmer**
darling **sevgili**
data (*information*) **data**
date (*day*) **tarih**
(*fruit*) **hurma**
daughter **kız çocuk**
daughter-in-law **gelin**
day **gün**
day after tomorrow
öbür gün
day before yesterday
önceki gün
the day after **ertesi
gün**
the day before **önceki
gün**
dead **ölü**
deaf **sağır**
dear **sevgili**
(*expensive*) **pahalı**

death **ölüm**
debt **borç**
decaffeinated **kafeinsiz**
deck **güverte**
deckchair **şezlong**
to decide **karar vermek**
to declare **açıklamak**
deep **derin**
deep-freeze **derin soğutucu**
deer **geyik**
defect **defo**
definitely! **muhakkak!**
to defrost **eritmek**
degree (*temperature*) **derece**
(*university*) **lisans**
delay **gecikme**
delicate **hassas**
delicious **lezzetli**
demonstration **gösteri**
dentist **dişçi**
dentures **takma diş**
deodorant **ter ilacı**
to depart **hareket etmek**
department **bölüm**
department store **mağaza**
departure **kalkış**
departure lounge **gidiş salonu**
deposit **depozito**

to describe **tarif etmek**
description **tarif**
desert **çöl**
design **desen**
to design **çizmek**
designer **çizimci**
dessert **tatlı**
destination **gidiş yeri**
detail **ayrıntı**
detergent **deterjan**
to develop (*film*) **develope etmek**
diabetes **şeker hastalığı**
to dial **çevirmek**
dialling code **kod numarası**
dialling tone **çevir sinyali**
diamond **pırlanta**
diarrhoea **diyare**
diary **not defteri**
dice **zar**
dictionary **sözlük**
to die **ölmek**
he/she/it died **öldü**
diesel **dizel**
diet **rejim**
to be on a diet **rejim yapmak**
different **değişik**
difficult **zor**
dining-room **yemek odası**

dinner **akşam yemeği**
dinner jacket **smokin**
diplomat **diplomat**
direct **direkt**
direction **istikamet**
directions **tarif**
director **müdür**
directory (*telephone*)
  telefon rehberi
dirty **kirli**
disabled **sakat**
disc **disk**
disco **diskotek**
discount **indirim**
dish (*course*) **yemek**
dishwasher **bulaşık
  makinesi**
disinfectant **dezanfektan**
dislocated **yerinden
  çıkmış**
disposable nappies
  kağıt çocuk bezi
distance **mesafe**
distilled water **arıtılmış
  su**
district **bölge**
to dive **dalmak**
  diving board **atlama
  tahtası**
divorced **boşanmış**
to do **yapmak**
  doctor **doktor**

document **belge**
dog **köpek**
doll **bebek**
dollar **dolar**
dome **kubbe**
donkey **eşek**
door **kapı**
double **çift**
  (*measure*) **duble**
double bed **iki kişilik
  yatak**
dough **hamur**
downstairs **aşağı kat**
drain **oluk**
draught (*of air*) **cereyan**
  (*beer*) **fıçı birası**
to draw **çizmek**
drawer **çekmece**
drawing **resim**
dreadful **korkunç**
dress **elbise**
to dress **giyinmek**
dressing (*medical*) **sargı**
  (*salad*) **sos**
drink **içki**
to drink **içmek**
to drive **araba kullanmak**
driver **şoför**
driving licence **ehliyet**
to drown **boğulmak**
drowned **boğulmuş**
drug **ilaç**

drug addict **esrarkeş**
drum **davul**
drunk **sarhoş**
dry **kuru**
dry-cleaner's **kuru temizleyici**
dubbed **dublajlı**
duck **ördek**
dumb **dilsiz**
during **sırasında**
dust **toz**
dustbin **çöp tenekesi**
dusty **tozlu**
duty (*customs*) **gümrük vergisi**
duty-free **gümrük vergisiz**
duvet **yorgan**

E

each **her**
ear **kulak**
earache **kulak ağrısı**
earlier (*before*) **daha önce**
early **erken**
to earn **kazanmak**
earring **küpe**
earth **dünya**
earthquake **deprem**
east **doğu**

eastern **doğulu**
Easter **Paskalya**
easy **kolay**
to eat **yemek**
economical **ekonomik**
economy, economics **ekonomi**
Edinburgh **Edimburg**
egg **yumurta**
either ... or **ya ... ya**
elastic band **lastik bant**
election **seçim**
electric **elektrik**
electrician **elektrikçi**
electricity **elektrik**
electronic **elektronik**
else: everything else **başka herşey**
embarrassing **utandırıcı**
embassy **büyükelçilik**
emergency **acil**
emergency exit **imdat çıkışı**
empty **boş**
to empty **boşaltmak**
enamel **mineli**
end **son**
  to come to an end **bitmek**
  to bring something to an end **bitirmek**
energetic **enerjik**

engaged (*to be married*) **nişanlı**

(*occupied*) **dolu**

engine **motor**

engineer **mühendis**

engineering **mühendislik**

England **İngiltere**

English **İngiliz**

enough **yeter**

to enter **girmek**

entertainment **eğlence**

enthusiastic **hevesli**

entrance **giriş**

envelope **zarf**

environment **çevre**

equal **eşit**

equipment **malzeme**

escalator **yürüyen merdiven**

especially **özellikle**

essential **şart**

estate agent **komisyoncu**

evaporated milk **kondanse süt**

even (*including*) **bile**

(*not odd*) **çift**

evening **akşam**

evening dress **gece elbisesi**

every **her**

everyone **herkes**

everything **herşey**

everywhere **heryer**

exactly **tam**

examination **imtihan**

example **örnek**

for example **örneğin**

excellent **fevkalade**

except **dışında**

excess luggage **fazla bagaj**

exchange **kambiyo**

exchange rate **kur**

excited **heyecanlı**

exciting **heyecanlı**

excursion **gezi**

excuse me! **affedersiniz!**

executive **yönetici**

exercise (*physical*) **jimnastik**

exhibition **sergi**

exit **çıkış**

to expect **beklemek**

expensive **pahalı**

experience **deneyim**

expert **uzman**

to explain **anlatmak**

explosion **patlama**

export **ihraç**

to export **ihraç etmek**

extension **iç numara**

external **dış**

extra (*in addition*) **fazladan**

eye **göz**
eyebrow **kaş**
eyebrow pencil **kaş kalemi**
eyelash **kirpik**
eyeliner **göz kalemi**
eyeshadow **göz boyası**

F

fabric **kumaş**
face **yüz**
face cream **yüz kremi**
face powder **pudra**
fact **gerçek**
  in fact **gerçekten**
factory **fabrika**
to fail (*exam, test*) **kalmak**
to faint **bayılmak**
fainted **baygın**
fair (*hair*) **sarışın**
fair **fuar**
  trade fair **sanayi fuarı**
fairly (*quite*) **oldukça**
faith **inanç**
faithful **sadık**
fake **yalancı**
to fall **düşmek**
false **sahte**
false teeth **takma diş**
family **aile**
famous **ünlü**

fan **yelpaze**
  (*electric*) **vantilatör**
  (*supporter*) **taraftar**
far (away) **uzak**
  is it far? **uzak mı?**
fare **bilet parası**
farm **çiftlik**
farmer **çiftçi**
fashion **moda**
fashionable/in fashion **moda**
fast **hızlı**
fat **yağ**
fat (*person, etc.*) **şişman**
father **baba**
father-in-law **kayınpeder**
fault (*defect*) **defo**
favourite **favori**
feather **tüy**
fed up **bıkkın**
  to be fed up **bıkmak**
to feed **yedirmek**
to feel **hissetmek**
  I feel well **iyiyim**
  I don't feel well **iyi değilim**
felt-tip pen **keçe uçlu kalem**
female, feminine **dişi**
feminist **feminist**
fence **çit**

ferry **vapur**
  car ferry **araba vapuru**
festival **festival**
fever **ateş**
few **az**
  a few **bir kaç**
fiancé(e) **nişanlı**
field **tarla**
fig **incir**
fight **kavga**
file **dosya**
  (*nail*) **törpü**
to fill (up) **doldurmak**
filling **dolgu**
film **filim**
film star **filim yıldızı**
filter **filtre**
finance **finans**
to find **bulmak**
fine **ince**
  (*weather*) **güzel**
  (*penalty*) **ceza**
to finish **bitirmek**
fire **ateş**
  (*conflagration*) **yangın**
fire brigade **itfaiye**
fire extinguisher **yangın söndürücü**
firewood **odun**
fireworks **havai fişek**
firm (*company*) **şirket**
first **ilk**

first aid **ilk yardım**
first aid box **ilk yardım çantası**
fish **balık**
to fish **balık tutmak**
fishing rod **olta**
fishmonger's **balıkçı**
to fit **uymak**
  it doesn't fit **uymuyor**
fitting room **soyunma odası**
to fix **tamir etmek**
fizzy **köpüklü**
flag **bayrak**
flat (*apartment*) **daire**
flat (*level*) **düz**
  (*battery*) **boş**
flavour **tad**
flaw **defo**
flea **pire**
flight **uçuş**
flight bag **uçak çantası**
flippers **palet**
flood **sel**
floor **yer**
floor (*storey*) **kat**
  ground floor **zemin kat**
flour **un**
flower **çiçek**
flu **grip**
fluid **sıvı**

fly **sinek**	freckle **çil**
foam **köpük**	free **serbest**
fog **sis**	freedom **hürriyet**
foggy **sisli**	to freeze **dondurmak**
foil **yaldız kağıt**	freezer **derin soğutucu**
folding chair **kapanan iskemle**	frequent **sık**
following (*next*) **izleyen**	fresh **taze**
food **yemek**	fridge **buzdolabı**
food poisoning **gıda zehirlenmesi**	fried **kızarmış**
foot **ayak**	friend **arkadaş, dost**
on foot **yürüyerek**	to be frightened **korkmak**
football **futbol**	fringe (*of hair*) **kakül**
footpath **patika**	frog **kurbağa**
for **için**	from **-den/-dan/-tan/-ten** (*see page 158*)
forbidden **yasak**	front **ön**
foreign **yabancı**	in front of **önünde**
forest **orman**	front door **ön kapı**
to forget **unutmak**	frontier **hudut**
to forgive **affetmek**	frost **don**
fork **çatal**	frozen **donmuş**
form (*document*) **form**	fruit **meyve**
fortnight **on beş gün**	fruiterer's **manav**
forward **ileri**	frying pan **tava**
foundation **temel**	fuel **yakıt**
(*make-up*) **fondöten**	full **dolu**
fountain **çeşme**	full board **tam pansiyon**
foyer **giriş**	full up (*hotel etc.*) **dolu**
fracture **kırık**	funeral **cenaze töreni**
fragile **kırılacak eşya**	funfair **lunapark**
frankly **açıkça**	funny **komik**

fur **kürk**
furniture **mobilya**
further on **daha ileri**
fuse **sigorta**

G

gallery **galeri**
gambling **kumar**
game **oyun**
garage (*car repair*) **tamirhane**
(*car parking*) **garaj**
garden **bahçe**
gardener **bahçıvan**
garlic **sarmısak**
gas **gaz**
gas bottle/cylinder **gaz tüpü**
bottled gas **tüpgaz**
gastritis **gastrit**
gate **kapı**
general **genel**
(*military*) **general**
generous **cömert**
gentle **nazik**
gentleman **bey**
genuine **gerçek**
geography **coğrafya**
to get **almak**
to get off **inmek**
to get on **binmek**

gift **hediye**
gin **cin**
gin and tonic **cin tonik**
girl **kız**
girlfriend **kızarkadaş**
to give **vermek**
can you give me ...? **bana ... verir misiniz?**
glass **bardak**
(*material*) **cam**
glasses **gözlük**
glove **eldiven**
glue **zamk**
to go **gitmek**
let's go **gidelim**
to go down **aşağı inmek**
to go in **girmek**
to go out **çıkmak**
to go up **yukarı çıkmak**
goal **gol**
goat **keçi**
God **Allah**
gold **altın**
goldsmith's **kuyumcu**
good **iyi**
good afternoon **iyi günler**
good evening **iyi akşamlar**
good morning **günaydın**

goodbye (*if you're leaving*) **Allahaısmarladık** (*if you're staying*) **güle güle**
government **hükümet**
gram **gram**
grammar **gramer**
grandchild **torun**
grandfather **büyükbaba**
grandmother **büyükanne**
grape **üzüm**
grapefruit **greyfrut**
grass **çim**
greasy **yağlı**
great **büyük**
  great! **çok iyi!**
Great Britain **Büyük Britanya**
green **yeşil**
greengrocer's **manav**
to greet **selamlamak**
grey **gri**
grilled **ızgara**
grocer's **bakkal**
ground **yer**
ground floor **zemin kat**
group **grup**
to grow **yetiştirmek**
guarantee **garanti**
guest **misafir**
guest house **pansiyon**

guide **rehber**
guidebook **rehber**
guided tour **rehberli tur**
guilty **suçlu**
gun **silah**
gymnastics **jimnastik**

H

habit **alışkanlık**
haemorrhoids **emoroit**
hair **saç**
  hairbrush **saç fırçası**
  haircut: to have a haircut **saçını kestirmek**
hairdresser's **berber, kuaför**
hairdrier **saç kurutma makinesi**
hairgrip **toka**
hairspray **saç spreyi**
half **yarım**
half an hour **yarım saat**
half board **yarım pansiyon**
half price **yarı fiat**
hall (*in a house*) **hol** (*concert*) **konser salonu**
hamburger **köfte**
hammer **çekiç**

hand **el**
handbag **çanta**
hand cream **el kremi**
handicapped **sakat**
handkerchief **mendil**
handle **sap**
   (*door*) **kapı kolu**
to hang **asmak**
to hang up (*phone*)
   kapatmak
to happen **olmak**
happy **mutlu**
harbour **liman**
hard **sert**
hard (*difficult*) **zor**
hat **şapka**
to hate **nefret etmek**
hayfever **saman nezlesi**
hazelnut **fındık**
he **o** (*see page 159*)
head **baş**
headache **başağrısı**
headphones **kulaklık**
to heal **iyileşmek**
health **sağlık**
healthy **sağlıklı**
to hear **duymak**
heart **kalp**
heart attack **kalp krizi**
heat **sıcaklık**
heater **ısıtıcı**
heating **kalorifer**

heaven **cennet**
heavy **ağır**
hedge **çit**
heel **topuk**
height **yükseklik**
helicopter **helikopter**
hell **cehennem**
hello! **merhaba!**
help! **imdat!**
to help **yardım etmek**
her **onu** (*see page 159*)
   (*of her*) **onun** (*see
   page 161*)
herb **ot**
here **burada**
hers **onun** (*see page
   161*)
hiccups **hıçkırık**
high **yüksek**
high-chair **çocuk
   iskemlesi**
to hijack **kaçırmak**
hill **tepe**
him **onu** (*see page 159*)
to hire **kiralamak**
his **onun** (*see page 161*)
history **tarih**
to hit **vurmak**
to hitch-hike **otostop
   yapmak**
hobby **hobi**
hole **delik**

holiday **tatil**
  on holiday **tatilde**
  public holiday **resmi tatil**
holy **kutsal**
home **ev**
  at home **evde**
  to go home **eve gitmek**
home address **ev adresi**
homosexual **eşcinsel**
honest **dürüst**
honeymoon **balayı**
to hope **ummak**
  I hope so **umarım**
horrible **felaket**
horse **at**
hose **hortum**
hospital **hastane**
hot **sıcak**
  (*spicy*) **acı**
  I'm hot **yanıyorum**
  it's hot (*weather*) **hava sıcak**
hotel **otel**
hour **saat**
house **ev**
housewife **ev kadını**
how **nasıl**
  how are you? **nasılsınız?**
  how many? **kaç?**
  how much? **kaç?**
  how much is it? **kaç para?**

human being **insan**
hungry **aç**
  to be hungry **acıkmak**
  I am hungry **acıktım**
to hunt **avlanmak**
hunting **av**
hurry: to be in a hurry **acele etmek**
hurt: my ... hurts **... ağrıyor** (*see page 138*)
husband **koca**
hut **kulübe**

I

I **ben** (*see page 159*)
ice **buz**
ice-cream **dondurma**
icy **buzlu**
idea **fikir**
if **eğer**
ill **hasta**
illness **hastalık**
to imagine **hayal etmek**
imagination **hayal gücü**
immediately **derhal**
immersion heater **ısıtıcı**
impatient **sabırsız**
important **önemli**
impossible **imkansız**
in **-de/-da/-te/-ta** (*see page 158*)

income **gelir**
independent **bağımsız**
indigestion **hazımsızlık**
indoors **içeride**
industrial **sınai**
industry **sanayi**
infected **hastalıklı**
infection **enfeksiyon**
inflammation **iltihap**
influenza **grip**
informal **gayriresmi**
information **bilgi**
information office
　danışma bürosu
injection **iğne**
injured **yaralı**
injury **yara**
ink **mürekkep**
inner **iç**
innocent **suçsuz**
insect bite **böcek ısırığı**
insecticide **böcek ilacı**
insect repellent
　böcekleri uzaklaştıran
　ilaç
inside **iç**
to insist **ısrar etmek**
instant coffee **neskahve**
instead of ... **... yerine**
instructor **öğretmen**
insulin **insulin**
insult **hakaret**

to insult **hakaret etmek**
insurance **sigorta**
insurance certificate
　sigorta sertifikası
intelligent **akıllı**
interested: to be
　interested **ilgilenmek**
interesting **enteresan**
interior **iç**
internal **dahili**
international **uluslarası**
interpreter **tercüman**
interval **ara**
interview **görüşme**
to introduce **tanıştırmak**
invitation **davetiye**
to invite **davet etmek**
iodine **tentürdiyot**
Ireland **İrlanda**
Irish **İrlandalı**
iron (*metal*) **demir**
　(*for clothes*) **ütü**
to iron **ütülemek**
ironmonger's **demirci**
is: he/she/it is (*see page 167*)
Islam **İslam**
Islamic **İslami**
island **ada**
it **o; onu** (*see page 159*)
itch **kaşıntı**
its **onun** (*see page 161*)

249

J

jacket **ceket**
jam **reçel**
jar **kavanoz**
jazz **caz**
jeans **blucin**
jelly **jöle**
jellyfish **denizanası**
Jesus **İsa**
jeweller's **mücevherci**
jewellery **mücevher**
Jewish **Yahudi**
job **iş**
jogging: to go jogging
  koşmak
joke **şaka**
journalist **gazeteci**
journey **yolculuk**
judge **hakim**
jug **sürahi**
juice **su**
to jump **atlamak**
jumper **kazak**
junction **kavşak**
just (*only*) **sadece**

K

to keep **saklamak**
kettle **çaydanlık**
key **anahtar**

key ring **anahtarlık**
kidney **böbrek**
to kill **öldürmek**
kilo(gram) **kilo(gram)**
kilometre **kilometre**
kind (*sort*) **çeşit**
  (*helpful*) **nazik**
king **kral**
kiss **öpücük**
to kiss **öpmek**
kitchen **mutfak**
knickers **don**
knife **bıçak**
to knit **örmek**
to knock **vurmak**
knot **düğüm**
to know (*someone*)
  tanımak
  (*something*) **bilmek**
  I know **biliyorum**
  I don't know
  bilmiyorum
Koran **Kuran**

L

label **etiket**
lace (*cloth*) **dantel**
  (*shoe*) **ayakkabı bağı**
ladder **merdiven**
lady **hanım**
  ladies and gentlemen
  baylar, bayanlar

lake **göl**
lamb **kuzu**
lamp **lamba**
lamp post **sokak lambası**
land **toprak**
to land **karaya çıkmak**
landlady **evsahibesi**
landlord **evsahibi**
lane **ara yol**
language **dil**
large **büyük**
last **son**
to last **sürmek**
late **geç**
later **daha sonra**
to laugh **gülmek**
laundry **çamaşır**
(place) **çamaşırhane**
law **kanun**
lawn **çimen**
lawyer **avukat**
laxative **laksatif**
lazy **tembel**
lead **kurşun**
lead-free **kurşunsuz**
leaf **yaprak**
leaflet **broşür**
to learn **öğrenmek**
learner **öğrenci**
least: at least **en az**
leather **deri**

to leave **bırakmak**
(depart) **ayrılmak**
left **sol**
on/to the left **sola**
left luggage (office) **emanet**
left-handed **solak**
leg **bacak**
legal **kanuni**
lemon **limon**
lemonade **limonata**
to lend **ödünç vermek**
length **uzunluk**
lens **lenz**
less **daha az**
lesson **ders**
to let (allow) **izin vermek**
(rent) **kiraya vermek**
letter **mektup**
(alphabet) **harf**
letterbox **mektup kutusu**
lettuce **yeşil salata**
level **düz**
level crossing **tren geçidi**
library **kütüphane**
licence (driving) **ehliyet**
lid **kapak**
life **hayat**
lifebelt **can yeleği**
lift **asansör**
to lift **kaldırmak**

light ışık
light (*in colour*) açık
　(*in weight*) hafif
to light yakmak
light bulb ampül
lighter çakmak
lightning şimşek
like (*similar to*) ... gibi
to like beğenmek
likely olası
line hat
lion arslan
lipstick dudak boyası
liqueur likör
liquid sıvı
liquor içki
list liste
to listen dinlemek
litre litre
litter çöp
a little çok az
to live (*exist*) yaşamak
　(*to reside*) oturmak
liver karaciğer
living-room oturma
　odası
loaf ekmek
local yerel
lock kilit
to lock kilitlemek
London Londra
long uzun

to look bakmak
to look after bakmak
to look for aramak
to look like benzemek
lorry kamyon
lorry-driver kamyon
　şoförü
to lose kaybetmek
lost property office
　kayıp eşya bürosu
a lot of çok
lotion losyon
lottery piyango
loud yüksek sesli
lounge salon
love sevgi
to love sevmek
lovely çok güzel
low alçak
lozenge pastil
LP uzunçalar
lucky şanslı
luggage bagaj
lump sugar kesme şeker
lunch öğle yemeği

M

machine makine
mad deli
madam hanımefendi
magazine mecmua

mail **posta**
make (*brand*) **marka**
to make **yapmak**
make-up **makyaj**
male **erkek**
man **adam**
manager **müdür**
managing director **genel müdür**
many **çok**
  not many **az**
map **harita**
marble **mermer**
margarine **margarin**
market **pazar**
married **evli**
mascara **rimel**
match (*game*) **maç**
matches **kibrit**
material (*cloth*) **kumaş**
mathematics **matematik**
matter: it doesn't matter **boş ver**
  what's the matter? **ne var?**
mattress **yatak**
mature **olgun**
mayonnaise **mayonez**
me **beni** (*see page 159*)
meal **yemek**
mean: what does it mean? **ne demek?**

meanwhile **bu arada**
measles **kızamık**
  German measles **kızamıkçık**
to measure **ölçmek**
measurement **ölçü**
meat **et**
  cold meats **soğuk etler**
mechanic **tamirci**
medical **tıbbi**
medicine (*subject*) **tıp** (*drug*) **ilaç**
Mediterranean **Akdeniz**
medium **orta**
meeting **toplantı**
melon **kavun**
  water melon **karpuz**
member **üye**
to mend **tamir etmek**
menu **mönü**
  set menu **tabldot**
message **mesaj**
metal **madeni**
metre **metre**
midday **öğle**
middle **orta**
middle-aged **orta yaşlı**
midnight **gece yarısı**
migraine **migren**
milk **süt**
mill **değirmen**
mince **kıyma**

mind: I don't mind **fark etmez**
mine **benim, benimki** (*see page 161*)
minister **bakan**
minute (*time*) **dakika**
mirror **ayna**
Miss **Bayan**
to miss (*bus, etc.*) **kaçırmak**
mistake **yanlış**
mixed **karışık**
mixture **karışım**
model **model**
modern **modern**
moisturiser **nemlendirici**
monastery **manastır**
money **para**
month **ay**
monument **yapıt**
moon **ay**
more **daha**
morning **sabah**
mortgage **ipotek**
mosque **cami**
mosquito **sivrisinek**
most (of) **çoğu**
mother **anne**
mother-in-law **kayınvalide**
motorbike **motorsiklet**
motorboat **motor**

motor racing **araba yarışı**
motorway **otoyol**
mountain **dağ**
mountaineering **dağcılık**
moustache **bıyık**
mouth **ağız**
to move **hareket etmek**
to move house **taşınmak**
movement **hareket**
Mr **Bay**
Mrs **Bayan**
much **çok**
not much **az**
to murder **öldürmek**
museum **müze**
mushroom **mantar**
music **müzik**
musical **müzikal**
musician **müzisyen**
Muslim **Müslüman**
mustard **hardal**
my **benim** (*see page 161*)

N

nail **çivi**
nail (*finger, toe*) **tırnak**
nail file **törpü**
nail polish **tırnak cilası**
nail polish remover **aseton**

naked **çıplak**
name **isim**
  my name is ... **ismim ...**
  what's your name?
   isminiz ne?
napkin **peçete**
  paper napkin **kağıt**
   peçete
nappy **çocuk bezi**
narrow **dar**
national **ulusal**
nationality **vatandaşlık**
natural **tabii**
navy **deniz kuvvetleri**
navy blue **lacivert**
near (to) **yakın**
nearly **hemen hemen**
necessary **lazım**
necklace **kolye**
needle **iğne**
negative **olumsuz**
negative (*photo*) **negatif**
neighbour **komşu**
neither ... nor ... **ne ...**
  ne ...
nephew **yeğen**
never **hiç bir zaman**
new **yeni**
New Testament **İncil**
New Year **Yeni Yıl**
news **haberler**
newspaper **gazete**

next **gelecek**
nice **güzel**
niece **yeğen**
night **gece**
night club **gece kulübü**
nightdress **gecelik**
no **hayır**
nobody **hiç kimse**
noise **gürültü**
noisy **gürültülü**
non-alcoholic **alkolsüz**
none **hiç bir**
non-smoking **sigara**
  içilmez
normal **normal**
north **kuzey**
northern **kuzey**
nose **burun**
not **değil**
note (*bank*) **kağıt para**
nothing **hiç bir şey**
nothing else **başka hiç**
  bir şey
now **şimdi**
nowhere **hiç bir yerde**
nuclear **nükleer**
nuclear energy **nükleer**
  enerji
number **sayı**
nurse **hastabakıcı**
nut **fıstık**
nylon **naylon**

oar **kürek**
object **şey**
occasionally **bazen**
occupied (*seat*) **dolu**
odd **tuhaf**
  (*not even*) **tek**
of course **tabii**
off: switched off **kapalı**
office **büro**
official (*noun*) **memur**
  (*adjective*) **resmi**
often **sık sık**
oil **yağ**
OK **tamam**
old (*things*) **eski**
  (*people*) **yaşlı**
  how old are you? **kaç**
  yaşındasınız?
  how old is he/she?
  kaç yaşında?
  I'm ... years old
  ... yaşındayım
olive **zeytin**
olive oil **zeytinyağı**
on **-de/-da/-te/-ta** (*see*
  page 158)
  switched on **açık**
once **bir defa**
onion **soğan**

only **yalnız**
open **açık**
to open **açmak**
opera **opera**
operation **ameliyat**
opinion **görüş**
  in my opinion **bence**
opposite (*contrary*) **zıt**
opposite (*to*) **karşı**
optician **gözlükçü**
or **veya**
orange **portakal**
orange-coloured
  portakal rengi
to order (*in restaurant*)
  ısmarlamak
ordinary **sıradan**
to organise **düzenlemek**
original **orijinal**
other **başka**
others **başkaları**
our **bizim** (*see page*
  161)
ours **bizim, bizimki** (*see*
  page 161)
outside **dışarı**
over (*above*) **üstünde**
overcast **kapalı**
overcoat **palto**
to overtake **sollamak**
owner **sahib**

P

package tour **tur**
packet **paket**
padlock **asma kilit**
page **sayfa**
pain **ağrı**
painkiller **ağrı kesici**
paint **boya**
to paint **boyamak**
painter **boyacı**
painting (*picture*) **resim**
pair **çift**
palace **saray**
pale (*colour*) **açık**
panties **don**
pants (*underpants*) **don**
paper **kağıt**
paper clip **ataş**
paraffin **parafin**
parcel **paket**
pardon? **efendim?**
parents **anne baba**
park **park**
to park **park etmek**
parliament **parlamento**
part **parça**
parting (*in hair*) **ayrık**
partly **kısmen**
partner **ortak**
party **parti**
to pass **geçmek**

passenger **yolcu**
passport **pasaport**
past **geçmiş**
pasta **makarna**
pastille **pastil**
pastry **hamur**
path **yol**
patient (*hospital*) **hasta**
pattern **desen**
pavement **kaldırım**
to pay **ödemek**
to pay cash **nakit para vermek**
pea **bezelye**
peace **barış**
peach **şeftali**
peanut **yer fıstığı**
pear **armut**
pedal **pedal**
pedestrian **yaya**
pedestrian crossing **yaya geçidi**
to peel **soymak**
peg **mandal**
pen **dolma kalem**
pencil **kurşun kalem**
pencil sharpener **kalemtraş**
penfriend **mektup arkadaşı**
penknife **çakı**
pension (*retirement*) **emeklilik**

pensioner **emekli**
people **insanlar**
  (*nation*) **millet**
pepper **biber**
  green pepper **yeşil biber**
  red pepper **kırmızı biber**
peppermint (*herb*) **nane**
  (*sweet*) **nane şekeri**
performance (*cinema*) **seans**
perfume **parfüm**
perhaps **belki**
period (*menstrual*) **aybaşı**
period pains **aybaşı ağrısı**
perm **perma**
permit (*noun*) **izin**
to permit **izin vermek**
person **şahıs**
personal **özel**
petrol **benzin**
petrol station **benzin istasyonu**
philosophy **felsefe**
photocopy **fotokopi**
to photocopy **fotokopi çekmek**
photograph **fotoğraf**

to photograph **fotoğraf çekmek**
photographer **fotoğrafçı**
photography **fotoğrafçılık**
phrase book **dil kılavuzu**
physics **fizik**
piano **piyano**
to pick (*choose*) **seçmek**
  (*flowers etc.*) **toplamak**
to pick up **almak**
picnic **piknik**
picture **resim**
piece **parça**
pier **iskele**
pig **domuz**
pill **hap**
  (*contraceptive*) **doğum kontrol hapı**
pillow **yastık**
pillowcase **yastık yüzü**
pilot **pilot**
pin **toplu iğne**
pineapple **ananas**
pink **pembe**
pipe (*for smoking*) **pipo**
  (*drain etc.*) **boru**
place **yer**
to place **koymak**
plan (*of town*) **harita**

plant **bitki**
plaster (*sticking*) **flaster**
plastic **plastik**
plastic bag **naylon torba**
plate **tabak**
platform (*station*) **peron**
play (*at a theatre*) **piyes**
to play (*instrument, record*)
  çalmak
  (*sport*) **oynamak**
pleasant **hoş**
please **lütfen**
pleased **memnun**
plenty (of) **çok**
pliers **kerpeten**
plug (*bath etc.*) **tıpa**
  (*electrical*) **fiş**
plumber **su tesisatçısı**
pneumonia **zatürree**
pocket **cep**
point **nokta**
poison **zehir**
poisonous **zehirli**
police **polis**
police car **polis arabası**
police station **karakol**
polish (*shoe etc.*) **cila**
polite **nazik**
political **siyasal**
politician **politikacı**
politics **siyaset**
polluted **kirli**

pollution **kirlilik**
pool (*swimming*) **havuz**
poor **fakir**
pop music **pop müziği**
Pope **Papa**
popular **sevilen**
pork **domuz eti**
port **liman**
portable **portatif**
porter **hamal**
portrait **portre**
possible **mümkün**
  as ... as possible
    mümkün olduğu
    kadar ...
  if possible **mümkünse**
possibly **olabilir**
post (*mail*) **posta**
postbox **posta kutusu**
postcard **kartpostal**
postcode **posta kodu**
postman **postacı**
post office **postane**
to postpone **ertelemek**
pot (*saucepan*) **tencere**
potato **patates**
pottery **seramik**
potty (*child's*) **lazımlık**
pound sterling **sterlin**
to pour **dökmek**
powder **pudra**
power **kuvvet**
  (*electrical*) **cereyan**

power cut **elektrik kesintisi**
pram **çocuk arabası**
to prefer **tercih etmek**
I prefer **tercih ediyorum**
pregnant **hamile**
to prepare **hazırlamak**
prescription **reçete**
present (*gift*) **hediye**
pretty **güzel**
price **fiyat**
priest (*Christian*) **papaz**
prime minister **başbakan**
prince **prens**
princess **prenses**
prison **hapishane**
private **özel**
prize **ödül**
probable **olası**
probably **herhalde**
problem **problem**
producer (*radio/TV*) **yapımcı**
profession **meslek**
professor **profesör**
profit **kâr**
programme **program**
prohibited **yasak**
to promise **söz vermek**
promise **söz**

to pronounce **telaffuz etmek**
properly **doğru**
property **mülk**
protestant **protestan**
province **il**
public **kamu**
public holiday **resmi tatil**
to pull **çekmek**
puncture **lastik patlaması**
pure **öz**
purple **mor**
purse **cüzdan**
to push **itmek**
push-chair **puset**
to put, put down **koymak**
I put **koyuyorum**
he/she puts **koyuyor**
pyjamas **pijama**

Q

quality **kalite**
quarter **çeyrek**
(*of town*) **mahalle**
quay **rıhtım**
queen **kraliçe**
question **soru**
queue **kuyruk**
quick **çabuk**

quickly **çabuk**
quiet (*place*) **sessiz**
quite **oldukça**
Qur'an **Kuran**

R

rabbi **haham**
rabbit **tavşan**
rabies **kuduz**
race **yarış**
  (*ethnic*) **ırk**
racecourse/track **pist**
racing **yarış**
radio **radyo**
railway **demiryolu**
railway station **istasyon**
rain **yağmur**
to rain **yağmak**
  it's raining **yağmur yağıyor**
raincoat **pardösü**
rainy **yağmurlu**
to rape **ırza geçmek**
rare (*steak*) **az pişmiş**
raspberry **ahududu**
rather (*quite*) **oldukça**
raw **çiğ**
razor **traş makinesi**
  (*cut-throat*) **ustura**
razor blade **jilet**
to reach (*arrive at*) **varmak**
to read **okumak**

ready **hazır**
real **gerçek**
really **gerçekten**
rear **arka**
reason **sebep**
receipt **fatura**
reception **resepsiyon**
receptionist **resepsiyon memuru**
recipe **yemek tarifesi**
to recognise **tanımak**
to recommend **tavsiye etmek**
record **plak**
record-player **pikap**
red **kırmızı**
red wine **kırmızı şarap**
reduction **indirim**
refrigerator **buzdolabı**
refund **iade**
region **bölge**
to register (*a letter*) **taahhütlü göndermek**
registration number **kayıt numarası**
  (*car*) **plaka numarası**
relation (*family*) **akraba**
religion **din**
religious **dini**
to remain **kalmak**
to remember **hatırlamak**
  I remember **hatırlıyorum**

to remove **kaldırmak**
to rent **kiralamak**
rental **kira**
to repair **tamir etmek**
to repeat **tekrar etmek**
reply **cevap**
report (*business*) **rapor**
(*newspaper*) **haber**
to rescue **kurtarmak**
rescue team **kurtarma
ekibi**
reservation **rezervasyon**
to reserve **ayırmak**
reserved **ayrılmış**
responsible **sorumlu**
to rest **dinlenmek**
restaurant **restoran**
restaurant car **yemekli
vagon**
result **sonuç**
retired **emekli**
return (*ticket*) **gidiş
dönüş**
to return (*go back*) **geri
dönmek**
(*give back*) **geri
vermek**
reverse-charge call
ödemeli telefon
rheumatism **romatizma**
ribbon **şerit**
(*hair*) **kurdele**

rice **pirinç**
(*cooked*) **pilav**
to ride **binmek**
(*bike*) **bisiklete ...**
(*in car*) **arabaya ...**
(*horse*) **ata ...**
right (*opposite of left*)
sağ
(*correct*) **doğru**
on/to the right **sağa**
on the right-hand side
sağ tarafta
right: you are right
haklısınız
right-hand **sağ taraf**
rights (*human etc.*)
haklar
ring (*jewellery*) **yüzük**
ripe **olgun**
river **nehir**
road **yol**
roadworks **yol tamiratı**
roast **fırın**
to rob **soymak**
I've been robbed
soyuldum
robbery **soygun**
roof **çatı**
roof-rack **üst bagaj**
room **oda**
rope **halat**
rose **gül**

rosé (*wine*) **roze**
rotten **çürük**
rough (*sea*) **dalgalı**
round **yuvarlak**
roundabout (*motoring*)
  göbek
row (*of seats*) **sıra**
to row (*boat*) **kürek**
  çekmek
rowing boat **kayık**
rubber **lastik**
rubbish **çöp**
rubbish! **saçma!**
rucksack **sırt çantası**
rude **kaba**
ruins **harabeler**
ruler (*measuring*) **cetvel**
to run **koşmak**
rush hour **kalabalık**
  saatler
rusty **paslı**

S

safe (*strongbox*) **kasa**
safe **emniyetli**
safety pin **çengelli iğne**
sail **yelken**
sailing (*sport*) **yelken**
  sporu
sailing boat **yelkenli**
sailor **denizci**

salad **salata**
salami **salam**
sale **satış**
  (*reduced prices*)
  ucuzluk
salesman/woman **satıcı**
salmon **som balığı**
salt **tuz**
salty **tuzlu**
same **aynı**
sample **örnek**
sand **kum**
sandal **sandalet**
sandwich **sandöviç**
  toasted sandwich
  tost
sanitary towel **hijyenik**
  kadın bağı
sauce **sos**
saucepan **tencere**
sauna **sauna**
sausage **sosis**
to save (*rescue*) **kurtarmak**
  (*money*) **biriktirmek**
to say **demek**
  I say **diyorum**
  how do you say it?
  nasıl dersiniz?
scales **tartı**
scarf **eşarp**
scene (*view*) **manzara**
scenery **manzara**

scent **koku**
 (*perfume*) **parfüm**
school **okul**
science **bilim**
scientist **bilim adamı**
scientific **bilimsel**
scissors **makas**
score: final score **sonuç**
scorpion **akrep**
Scotland **İskoçya**
Scottish **İskoç**
scratch **çizik**
screen **perde**
screw **vida**
screwdriver **tornavida**
sculpture **heykel**
sea **deniz**
seafood **deniz mahsulleri**
seasickness **deniz
 tutması**
season **mevsim**
season ticket **abonman**
seat **yer**
seatbelt **kemer**
second (*numbers*) **ikinci**
second (*time*) **saniye**
secret **sır**
secretary **sekreter**
section **bölüm**
to see **görmek**
 I see (*understand*)
 anlıyorum

to seem **görünmek**
 it seems that ... **öyle
 görünüyor ki ...**
self-service **self servis**
to sell **satmak**
to send **göndermek**
sentence **cümle**
 (*legal*) **ceza**
separate **ayrı**
serious **ciddi**
 (*important*) **önemli**
to serve **hizmet etmek**
service **hizmet**
service charge **servis
 ücreti**
set (*group*) **takım**
 (*series*) **dizi**
 (*hair*) **mizanpili**
several **birkaç**
to sew **dikmek**
sewing **dikiş**
sex (*gender*) **cinsiyet**
 (*intercourse*) **cinsel
 ilişki**
shade (*colour*) **renk tonu**
shadow **gölge**
shampoo **şampuan**
shampoo and set
 yıkama ve mizanpili
shampoo and blow-dry
 yıkama ve fön
sharp **keskin**

to shave **traş olmak**
shaver **traş makinesi**
shaving cream **traş kremi**
she **o** (*see page 159*)
sheep **koyun**
sheet **çarşaf**
shell **kabuk**
shellfish **kabuklu deniz hayvanı**
shelter **barınak**
shiny **parlak**
ship **gemi**
shock **şok**
shoe **ayakkabı**
shoelace **ayakkabı bağı**
shoe polish **ayakkabı boyası**
shoe shop **ayakkabıcı**
shop **dükkan**
shop assistant **satıcı**
shopping **alış veriş**
to go shopping **alış verişe çıkmak**
shopping centre **alış veriş merkezi**
short **kısa**
shorts **şort**
to shout **bağırmak**
show **gösteri**
to show **göstermek**

shower **duş**
to have a shower **duş yapmak**
to shrink **çekmek**
shut **kapalı**
shutter **kepenk**
(*camera*) **objektif kapağı**
sick (*ill*) **hasta**
to be sick **kusmak**
to feel sick **midesi bulanmak**
I feel sick **midem bulanıyor**
side **kenar**
sieve **elek**
sight (*vision*) **görüş**
sights (*tourist*) **görülecek yer**
sightseeing **gezme**
sign **işaret**
to sign **imza etmek**
signal **sinyal**
signature **imza**
silent **sessiz**
silk **ipek**
silver **gümüş**
similar **benzer**
simple **basit**
since **-den/-dan/-ten/-tan beri**
to sing **şarkı söylemek**

single (*room, bed*) **tek**
  kişilik
  (*ticket*) **gidiş**
  (*unmarried*) **bekar**
sink **lavabo**
sister **kızkardeş**
  elder sister **abla**
sister-in-law (*wife's*
  sister) **baldız**
  (*husband's sister*)
  görümce
  (*brother's wife*) **yenge**
to sit/sit down **oturmak**
size (*dimension*)
  büyüklük
  (*clothes*) **beden**
  (*shoes*) **numara**
skates **paten**
to skate **paten yapmak**
ski **ski**
to ski **ski yapmak**
skimmed milk **yağsız**
  süt
skin **deri**
skirt **etek**
sky **gökyüzü**
sleep **uyku**
to sleep **uyumak**
sleeper/sleeping car
  yataklı vagon
sleeping bag **uyku**
  tulumu

sleeve **kol**
slice **dilim**
sliced **dilimlenmiş**
slide (*film*) **diya**
slim **ince**
slip (*petticoat*)
  kombinezon
slippery **kaygan**
slow **yavaş**
slowly **yavaş yavaş**
small **küçük**
smell **koku**
to smell **kokmak**
smile **gülümseme**
to smile **gülümsemek**
smoke **duman**
smoked (*food*) **füme**
smooth **düz**
snake **yılan**
to sneeze **hapşırmak**
snow **kar**
  it's snowing **kar**
  yağıyor
so **onun için**
  (*thus*) **böylece**
  so many/so much **çok**
soap **sabun**
socialism **sosyalism**
socialist **sosyalist**
sociology **sosyoloji**
sock **çorap**
socket (*electrical*) **priz**

soda (*water*) **soda**
soft **yumuşak**
soft drink **alkolsüz içki**
sold out **kalmadı**
soldier **asker**
solid **katı**
some **bazı**
somehow **nasılsa**
someone **birisi**
something **birşey**
sometimes **bazen**
somewhere **bir yerde**
son **oğul**
song **şarkı**
son-in-law **damat**
soon **yakında**
  as soon as possible **en kısa zamanda**
sore throat: I have a sore throat **boğazım ağrıyor**
sorry! **affedersiniz!**
sort (*type*) **çeşit**
sound **ses**
soup **çorba**
sour **ekşi**
south, southern **güney**
souvenir **hediye**
space **yer**
spade **kürek**
spanner **İngiliz anahtarı**

spare (*available*) **boş**
  (*left over*) **fazla**
  (*extra*) **yedek**
spare time **boş zaman**
spare tyre **yedek lastik**
spare wheel **yedek tekerlek**
sparkling (*wine*) **köpüklü**
to speak **konuşmak**
special **özel**
specialist **uzman**
speciality **özellik**
spectacles **gözlük**
speed **hız**
speed limit **azami hız**
to spend (*money*) **harcamak**
  (*time*) **vakit geçirmek**
spice **baharat**
spicy **baharatlı**
spinach **ıspanak**
spirits **alkollü içki**
to spoil **bozmak**
sponge **sünger**
spoon **kaşık**
sport **spor**
spot **nokta**
  (*stain*) **leke**
to sprain **burkmak**
to be sprained **burkulmak**
spring **ilkbahar**

square **meydan**
(*shape*) **kare**
stadium **stadyum**
stain **leke**
stainless steel **paslanmaz çelik**
stairs **merdiven**
stalls (*theatre*) **koltuk**
stamp **pul**
standing (up) **ayakta**
to stand **ayakta durmak**
to stand up **ayağa kalkmak**
staple **tel raptiye**
stapler **tel zımba**
star **yıldız**
start (*beginning*) **başlangıç**
to start **başlamak**
starter (*food*) **meze**
station **istasyon**
stationer's **kırtasiyeci**
statue **heykel**
to stay **kalmak**
steak **biftek**
to steal **çalmak**
steam **buhar**
steel **çelik**
steep **dik**
step **basamak**
stepchildren **üvey çocuk**
stepdaughter **üvey kız**

stepfather **üvey baba**
stepmother **üvey anne**
stepson **üvey oğul**
stereo **stereo**
sterling: pound sterling **sterlin**
steward (*air*) **kabin memuru**
stewardess (*air*) **hostes**
stick **sopa**
walking stick **baston**
to stick **yapışmak**
sticking plaster **flaster**
sticky **yapışkan**
sticky tape **yapışkan bant**
still **hala**
still (*non-fizzy*) **köpüksüz**
to sting **sokmak**
stock exchange **borsa**
stocking **çorap**
stolen: my ... has been stolen **... çalındı**
stomach **mide**
stomach ache **karın ağrısı**
stomach upset **mide bozukluğu**
stone **taş**
stop **durak**
to stop **durmak**
stop! **dur!**

stopcock **tıpa**
storey **kat**
story **öykü**
stove (*cooker*) **ocak**
straight **düz**
straight on **doğru**
strange **garip**
stranger (*unknown person*) **yabancı**
strap **bağ**
straw (*drinking*) **çubuk**
strawberry **çilek**
stream **dere**
street **sokak**
street light **sokak lambası**
stretcher **sedye**
strike **vuruş**
to strike **vurmak**
string **ip**
stripe **çizgi**
striped **çizgili**
strong **kuvvetli**
student **öğrenci**
to study **ders çalışmak**
stupid **aptal**
style **biçim**
to style **biçimlendirmek**
subtitled **alt yazılı**
suburb(s) **banliyö**
to succeed **başarmak**
success **başarı**

successful **başarılı**
suddenly **birdenbire**
sugar **şeker**
sugar lump **kesme şeker**
suit **takım elbise**
suitcase **bavul**
summer **yaz**
sun **güneş**
to sunbathe **güneşlenmek**
sunburn **güneş yanığı**
sunglasses **güneş gözlüğü**
sunshade (*beach*) **gölgelik**
sunstroke **güneş çarpması**
suntan cream **güneş kremi**
suntan oil **güneş yağı**
supermarket **süpermarket**
supper **akşam yemeği**
supplement **ek ücret**
suppose: I suppose so **herhalde**
suppository **fitil**
sure **emin**
surface **yüzey**
surname **soyadı**
surprise **sürpriz**
surprised **şaşkın**
surrounded (by) **çevrili**

sweat **ter**
sweater **kazak**
sweatshirt **penye**
to sweep **süpürge**
sweet **tatlı**
sweet (*dessert*) **tatlı**
sweets **şeker**
(*chocolates*) **çikolata**
(*toffees*) **karamela**
swelling **şiş**
to swim **yüzme**
swimming **yüzme**
swimming pool **yüzme havuzu**
swimming trunks, swimsuit **mayo**
switch **düğme**
to switch off **kapatmak**
to switch on **açmak**
swollen **şiş**
symptom **belirti**
synagogue **sinagog**
synthetic **sentetik**
system **sistem**

T

table **masa**
tablet **hap**
table tennis **masa tenisi**
tailor **terzi**
to take **almak**

to take (*a bus, etc.*) **...-(y)e binmek**
to take off (*remove*) **çıkarmak**
(*plane*) **kalkmak**
to take out **çıkarmak**
taken (*seat*) **dolu**
talcum powder **talk pudrası**
to talk **konuşmak**
tall (*people*) **uzun**
(*things*) **yüksek**
tampon **tampon**
tap **musluk**
tape **şerit, teyp**
tape measure **şerit metre**
tape recorder **ses alma makinesi, teyp**
taste **tat**
tasty **lezzetli**
tax **vergi**
taxi **taksi**
tea **çay**
teabag **torba çay**
to teach **öğretmek**
teacher **öğretmen**
team **ekip**
(*sports*) **takım**
teapot **demlik**
tear **gözyaşı**
to tear **yırtmak**

teaspoon **çay kaşığı**

tea-towel **kurulama bezi**

technical **teknik**

technology **teknik**

teenager (*female*)
  gençkız
  (*male*) **delikanlı**

telegram **telgraf**

telephone **telefon**

telephone directory
  telefon rehberi

television **televizyon**

to tell **söylemek**

temperature **ısı**
  I have a temperature
  ateşim var

temporary **geçici**

tender **hassas**

tennis **tenis**

tennis court **tenis kortu**

tennis shoes **tenis
  ayakkabısı**

tent **çadır**

tent peg **çadır çivisi**

tent pole **çadır direği**

terminal, terminus **son
  durak**

terrace **taraça**

terrible **çok kötü**

terrorist **terörist**

thank you (very much)
  (çok) teşekkür ederim

that, that one **şu, o** (*see
  page 163*)

theatre **tiyatro**

their **onların** (*see page
  161*)

them **onlar** (*see page
  159*)

then **sonra**

there **orada**

there is/are **... var**
  there is/are not **... yok**
  (*see page 169*)

therefore **onun için**

thermometer
  termometre, derece

these **bunlar** (*see page
  163*)

they **onlar** (*see page
  159*)

thief **hırsız**

thick **kalın**

thin **ince**

thing **şey**

to think **düşünmek**
  (*suppose*) **sanmak**
  I think so **sanıyorum**
  I don't think so
  sanmıyorum

third **üçüncü**

thirsty: to be thirsty
  susamak
  I am thirsty **susadım**

this, this one **bu** (*see page 163*)

those **şunlar, onlar** (*see page 163*)

thread **iplik**

throat **boğaz**

to throw **atmak**

thumb **başparmak**

thunder **gök gürültüsü**

ticket **bilet**

ticket office **gişe**

tidy **toplu**

tie **kravat**

to tie **bağlamak**

tight **sıkı**

tights **külotlu çorap**

till (*until*) **-e/-a/-ye/-ya kadar**

till (*cash*) **kasa**

time (*once, etc.*) **kere, defa**

time **saat** (*see page 173*)

there's no time **vakit yok**

timetable **tarife**

tin foil **yaldız kağıt**

tin opener **konserve açacağı**

tinned **konserve**

tip (*money*) **bahşiş**

tired **yorgun**

tissues **kağıt mendil**

to **-de/-da/-te/-ta** (*see page 158*)

toast **kızarmış ekmek**

toasted sandwich **tost**

tobacco **tütün**

today **bugün**

together **beraber**

toilet **tuvalet**

toilet paper **tuvalet kağıdı**

toilet water **kolonya**

tomato **domates**

tomorrow **yarın**

tongue **dil**

tonic water **tonik**

tonight **bu gece**

too (*also*) **-de/-da/-te/-ta**

too (*excessively*) **fazla**

tool **alet**

too many **çok**

too much **çok**

tooth **diş**

toothache **diş ağrısı**

toothbrush **diş fırçası**

toothpaste **diş macunu**

toothpick **kürdan**

top: on top of **üstünde**

top floor **üst kat**

torch **el feneri**

torn **yırtık**

total **toplam**

to touch **ellemek**

tough (*meat*) **sert**
tour **tur**
tourism **turizm**
tourist **turist**
tourist office **turizm bürosu**
to tow **çekmek**
towards **doğru**
towel **havlu**
tower **kule**
town **şehir**
town centre **şehir merkezi**
town hall **belediye**
tow rope **çekme halatı**
toy **oyuncak**
trade union **sendika**
traditional **geleneksel**
traffic **trafik**
traffic jam **trafik sıkışıklığı**
traffic lights **trafik ışıkları**
trailer **trayler**
train **tren**
  by train **trenle**
tranquilliser **sakinleştirici**
to translate **çevirmek**
translation **çeviri**
to travel **seyahat etmek**

travel agency **seyahat acentası**
traveller's cheque **seyahat çeki**
travel sickness **araç tutması**
tray **tepsi**
treatment **tedavi**
tree **ağaç**
trip **yolculuk**
trousers **pantolon**
trout **alabalık**
true: that's true **doğru**
to try **denemek**
to try on **prova etmek**
T-shirt **tişört**
tube **tüp**
tuna **ton balığı**
tunnel **tünel**
to turn **dönmek**
to turn off **kapamak**
to turn on **açmak**
turning (*side road*) **sapak**
twice **iki kere**
twin beds **çift yatak**
twins **ikizler**
type (*sort*) **çeşit**
to type **daktilo etmek**
typewriter **daktilo**
typical **tipik**

U

ugly **çirkin**
ulcer **ülser**
umbrella **şemsiye**
uncle **amca**
uncomfortable **rahatsız**
under **altında**
underground **metro**
underpants **külot**
to understand **anlamak**
  I understand
    anlıyorum
  I don't understand
    anlamıyorum
underwater **sualtı**
underwear **iç çamaşırı**
unemployed **işsiz**
unfortunately **maalesef**
unhappy **mutsuz**
uniform **üniforma**
university **üniversite**
unleaded petrol
  kurşunsuz benzin
unpleasant **hoş olmayan**
to unscrew **vidayı**
  çıkarmak
until **-e/-a/-ye/-ya kadar**
unusual **az görülen**
unwell **hasta**
up, upper **üst**
upstairs **üst kat**

urgent **acele**
urine **idrar**
us **bizi** (*see page 159*)
use **kullanım, fayda**
to use **kullanmak**
useful **faydalı**
useless **faydasız, işe**
  yaramaz
usual: as usual **her**
  zamanki gibi
usually **genellikle**

V

vacant **boş**
vacuum cleaner **elektrik**
  süpürgesi
vacuum flask **termos**
valid **geçerli**
valley **vadi**
valuable **kıymetli**
valuables **kıymetli eşya**
van **kamyonet**
vanilla **vanilya**
vase **vazo**
VAT **KDV**
veal **dana**
vegetable **sebze**
vegetarian **etyemez**
vehicle **araç**
vermouth **vermut**
very **çok**

very much **çok**
vest **fanila**
vet **veteriner**
via **yoluyla**
video cassette **video kaset**
video recorder **video**
view **manzara**
villa **villa**
village **köy**
  (*holiday*) **tatil köyü**
vinegar **sirke**
vine **asma**
vineyard **bağ**
virgin **bakire**
Virgin Mary **Meryem Ana**
visit **ziyaret**
to visit **ziyaret etmek**
visitor **ziyaretçi**
vitamin **vitamin**
vodka **votka**
voice **ses**
volleyball **voleybol**
voltage **voltaj**
vote **oy**
to vote **oy vermek**

W

wage **ücret**
waist **bel**

waistcoat **yelek**
to wait **beklemek**
waiter **garson**
Wales **Galler**
walk **yürüyüş**
  to go for a walk
    yürüyüşe çıkmak
to walk **yürümek**
walking stick **baston**
wall **duvar**
walls (*city*) **surlar**
wallet **cüzdan**
walnut **ceviz**
to want **istemek**
  would like: I would
  like **isterim**
war **savaş**
warm **ılık**
to wash **yıkamak**
washable **yıkanır**
wash-basin **lavabo**
washing **yıkama**
washing machine
  çamaşır makinesi
washing powder
  çamaşır tozu
washing-up **bulaşık**
  to do the washing up
    bulaşık yıkamak
washing-up liquid
  deterjan
wasp **eşek arısı**

wastepaper basket **çöp sepeti**

watch (*wristwatch*) **kol saati**

to watch **seyretmek**

water **su**

water-heater **su ısıtıcı**

water melon **kavun**

waterfall **şelale**

waterproof **sugeçirmez**

water-skiing **su kayağı**

wave **dalga**

wax **balmumu**

way **yol**

  that way **o taraf**

  this way **bu taraf**

way in **giriş**

way out **çıkış**

we **biz** (*see page 159*)

weather **hava**

  what's the weather like? **hava nasıl?**

wedding **düğün**

week **hafta**

weekdays **hafta arası**

weekend **hafta sonu**

weekly **haftalık**

  (*each week*) **her hafta**

to weigh **tartmak**

weight **ağırlık**

welcome **hoş geldiniz**

well (*for water*) **kuyu**

well **iyi**

I feel well **iyiyim**

I don't feel well **iyi değilim**

well done (*steak*) **iyi pişmiş**

Welsh **Galli**

west **batı**

western **batılı**

wet **ıslak**

what? **ne?**

wheel **tekerlek**

wheelchair **tekerlekli iskemle**

when? **ne zaman?**

where? **nerede?**

which? **hangi?**

while **sırasında**

whisky **viski**

whisky and soda **viski soda**

who? **kim?**

  who is it? **kim o?**

whole **bütün**

wholemeal bread **kepek ekmeği**

whose? **kimin?**

why? **niçin?**

wide **geniş**

widow, widower **dul**

wife **karı**

wild **yabani**

win **kazanç**
to win **kazanmak**
  who won? **kim kazandı?**
wind **rüzgar**
windmill **değirmen**
window **pencere**
  (*shop*) **vitrin**
windsurfing **rüzgar sörfü**
windy **rüzgarlı**
wing **kanat**
winter **kış**
with **ile; -le/-la/-yle/-yla** (*see page 158*)
without **-siz/-süz/-sız/ -suz** (*see page 158*)
woman **kadın**
wonderful **fevkalade**
wood (*trees*) **ağaçlık**
  (*material*) **tahta**
wool **yün**
word **kelime**
work **iş**
to work (*at job*) **çalışmak**
  (*function*) **işlemek**
world **dünya**
  First/Second World War **Birinci/İkinci Dünya Savaşı**
worry **merak**
  don't worry **merak etme**

worse **daha kötü**
worth **değer**
  it is worth it **değer**
  it isn't worth it **değmez**
wound (*injury*) **yara**
to wrap (up) **sarmak**
to write **yazmak**
writer **yazar**
writing paper **dosya kağıdı**
wrong (*incorrect*) **yanlış**

X

X-ray **röntgen**

Y

yacht **yat**
to yawn **esnemek**
year **yıl**
yellow **sarı**
yes **evet**
yesterday **dün**
yet **henüz**
  not yet **henüz değil**
yoghurt **yoğurt**
you (*informal*) **sen; seni**
  (*formal/plural*) **siz; sizi** (*see page 159*)
young **genç**

your **senin; sizin** (*see page 161*)

yours **senin; sizin** (*see page 161*)

youth **genç**

youth hostel **gençlik yurdu**

Z

zip **fermuar**

zoo **hayvanat bahçesi**

zoology **zooloji**

NOTES

NOTES

NOTES

NOTES

NOTES

EMERGENCIES

(*See also* Problems and complaints, *page* 147; Health, *page* 135)

You may want to say

Phoning the emergency services

The police, please
Polis lütfen
polis lewtfen

The fire brigade, please
İtfaiye lütfen
itfa:iye lewtfen

An ambulance, please
Bir ambulans lütfen
bir ambulans lewtfen

There's been a burglary
Bir hırsızlık oldu
bir huhrsuhzluhk olduh

There's been an accident
Bir kaza oldu
bir kaza: oldu

There's a fire
Yangın var
yanguhn var

I've been attacked/mugged
Bana saldırdılar
bana salduhrduhlar

I've been raped
Irzıma geçtiler
uhrzuhma gechtiler

There's someone injured/ill
Yaralı/Hasta var
yaraluh/hasta var

It's my husband/son
Kocam/Oğlum
kojam/o:lum

It's my wife/daughter
Karım/Kızım
karuhm/kuhzuhm

It's my friend
Arkadaşım
arkadashuhm

Please come immediately
Lütfen hemen gelin
lewtfen hemen gelin

I am at/at the ...
... deyim/... dayım
... deyim/... diyuhm

My name is ...
İsmim ...
ismim ...

My telephone number is ...
Telefon numaram ...
telefon numaram ...

Where is the police station?
Karakol nerede?
karakol nerede

Where is the hospital?
Hastane nerede?
hasta:ne nerede

At the police station/hospital

Is there anybody who
   speaks English?
İngilizce bilen var mı?
ingilizje bilen var muh

I want to speak to a woman
Bir kadınla konuşmak istiyorum
bir kaduhnla konushmak istiyorum

Please call the British Embassy
Lütfen İngiltere Büyükelçiliğini arayın
lewtfen ingiltere bewyewkelchili:ini ariyuhn

I want a lawyer
Bir avukat istiyorum
bir avukat istiyorum

You may hear

When you phone the emergency services

Mesele nedir?
mesele nedir
What's the matter?

Ne oldu?
ne oldu
What happened?

Adınızı ve adresinizi verin
aduhnuhzuh ve adresinizi verin
Give me your name and
   address

Hemen bir ekip yolluyoruz
hemen bir ekip yolluyoruz
We are sending a police
   patrol at once

Bir polis arabası yola çıkıyor
bir polis arabasuh yola chuhkuhyor
A police car is on the way

İtfaiye arabası yolda
itfa:iye arabasuh yolda
The fire engine is on the way

Hemen bir ambulans yolluyorum
hemen bir ambulans yolluyorum
I am sending an ambulance immediately

The police

Adınız ne?
aduhnuhz ne
What is your name?

Adresiniz ne?
adresiniz ne
What is your address?

Ne oldu?
ne oldu
What happened?

Nerede oldu?
nerede oldu
Where did it happen?

Ne zaman oldu?
ne zaman oldu
When did it happen?

... anlatır mısınız?
... anlatuhr muhsuhnuhz
Can you describe ...?

Benimle/Bizimle karakola gelin
benimle/bizimle karakola gelin
Come with me/with us to the police station

Tutuklusunuz
tutuklusunuz
You are under arrest

The doctor

Nereniz ağrıyor?
nereniz a:ruhyor
Where does it hurt?

Ne zamandan beri böyle?
ne zamandan beri böyle
Since when has it been like this?

Hastaneye gitmeniz lazım
hastaneye gitmeniz lazım
You have to go to hospital

Hastaneye gitmesi lazım
hastaneye gitmesi lazım
He/she/it has to go to hospital

Emergency shouts

Help!
İmdat!
imdat

Help me!
Yardım edin!
yarduhm edin

Police!
Polis!
polis

Stop!
Dur!
dur

Stop thief!
Durdurun hırsız!
durdurun huhrsuhz

Look out!
Dikkat!
dikkat

Fire!
Yangın var!
yanguhn var

Danger! Gas!
Tehlike var! Gaz!
tehlike var gaz

Get out of the way!
Çekilin!
chekilin

Call the police!
Polis çağırın!
polis cha:uhruhn

Call the fire brigade
İtfaiyeyi çağırın
itfa:iyeyi cha:uhruhn

Call an ambulance
Ambulans çağırın
ambulans cha:uhruhn

Get a doctor
Doktor çağırın
doktor cha:uhruhn

Get help quickly
Çabuk yardım çağırın
chabuk yarduhm cha:uhruhn

It's an emergency
Bu acil bir durum
bu a:jil bir durum

Emergency telephone numbers in Turkey

The emergency number for the police is generally 055, and for the ambulance 077, but these may vary in some areas. The best thing to do is to check the numbers wherever you're staying.

ALL-PURPOSE PHRASES

Hello
Merhaba
merhaba

Good day
İyi günler
iyi gewnler

Good morning
Günaydın
gewnayduhn

Good evening
İyi akşamlar
iyi akshamlar

Goodnight
İyi geceler
iyi gejeler

Goodbye (*if you're leaving*)
Allahaısmarladık
ala:smalduhk

Goodbye (*if you're staying*)
Güle güle
gewle gewle

Yes
Evet
evet

No
Hayır
hiyuhr

Please
Lütfen
lewtfen

Thank you (very much)
(Çok) teşekkür ederim
chok teshekkewr ederim

Don't mention it
Birşey değil
birshey de:il

I don't know
Bilmiyorum
bilmiyorum

I don't understand
Anlamıyorum
anlamuhyorum

I speak very little Turkish
Çok az Türkçe biliyorum
chok az tewrkche biliyorum

Pardon?
Efendim?
efendim

Could you repeat that?
Tekrarlar mısınız?
tekrarlar muhsuhnuhz

More slowly
Daha yavaş
daha yavash